Stevenage
History and Guide

Margaret Ashby

ALAN SUTTON PUBLISHING

First published in the United Kingdom in 1994
Alan Sutton Publishing Ltd
Phoenix Mill · Far Thrupp · Stroud · Gloucestershire

First published in the United States of America in 1994
Alan Sutton Publishing Inc.
83 Washington Street · Dover · NH 03820

British Library Cataloguing in Publication Data

A catalogue record for this book is available from the British Library.

ISBN 0–7509–0426–7

Library of Congress Cataloging in Publication Data applied for

Jacket illustration: St Nicholas' church *by Betty Game.*

Books by the Same Author

The Book of the River Lea
The Book of Stevenage
Forster Country

Typeset in 10/13 Times.
Typesetting and origination by
Alan Sutton Limited.
Printed in Great Britain by
The Bath Press, Avon.

Contents

CHAPTER ONE

The Romans

Two thousand years ago, in the first century BC when Hertfordshire was part of the territory of the ancient British Catevellauni and Trinovante tribes, the place now known as Stevenage was a tree-covered expanse, thinly populated by human beings, and home to wild boar, wolves and deer. In the forest of native trees, such as oak, hawthorn, holly and hornbeam, there were man-made clearings, often surrounded by fields and pasture land, where the Britons had built their dwellings.

When the Romans began colonizing England after AD 43, they established two of their most prominent cities, Londinium (London) and Verulamium (St Albans), within a day's march of Stevenage. From each of these two centres flowed a network of roads, many of which were existing prehistoric tracks now upgraded and straightened by Roman engineers. One, from Verulamium to the important Romano-British settlement and crossroads at Baldock, passed through Symond's Green, Fisher's Green, Corey's Mill and Graveley. Parts of it can still be walked as footpaths and the route of other sections can be traced in today's urban landscape.

But it was another Roman road which was to have a more far-reaching effect on the future town of Stevenage. This was the route from London to the north, which ran from the Roman fort at Cripplegate, through Southgate, Potters Bar, Brookman's Park, Woolmer Green and Stevenage and was later to achieve pre-eminence as the Great North Road, designated A1. Now demoted to a B road following the building of the A1(M) by-pass, which stole its thunder, the old Great North Road followed a perfectly straight line from the Roebuck Inn at Broadwater through Stevenage, where it became the High Street, to just beyond Corey's Mill, where it joined the Roman road from Verulamium to Baldock.

In building this magnificent road the Roman civil engineers opened up the adjacent land to settlers; pioneers who gradually spread further afield from the safety of the cities to make their homes among the native population whom they subdued with their superior weapons and disciplined troops. On either side of the

opposite, above:
archaeological excavation
work at Chells Manor Village
site in 1986; below: the hoard
of Roman coins found in 1986.

Roman road from London to the north, Roman settlements – the equivalent of modern 'developments' – grew up.

The Stevenage district was probably quite heavily populated by Roman colonists, although until recently comparatively little by way of archaeological remains had come to light. Some Roman artefacts, including a jug, some coins and pottery, were found in Sish Lane and some pottery fragments in Whomerley Wood. Another indication of a Roman presence is found in the previous name for Letchmore Road which, up to the sixteenth century was known as Letchmere Street. The use of the term 'street' in an old road is usually a sign that the road was built or used by the Romans. It is also interesting that Letchmore Road has apparently always followed its present straight course, suggestive of a probable Roman origin, although not all straight roads were Roman.

Some late Roman items were found in Broadwater in 1961, including fragments of tiles, pottery, glass, an iron knife, a bronze pin and a comb. Other evidence of a Roman presence in the district includes pottery and other items of the second and third centuries AD found near Wymondley Bury, indicating a sizeable settlement there.

During the autumn of 1986, when the modern new town of Stevenage was being extended eastwards by building on the fields between Chells and Walkern, a remarkable discovery was made. Archaeologists working on the site unearthed a pot containing about two thousand five hundred Roman coins. A full-scale investigation was then mounted by the Hertfordshire Archaeological Trust, at the invitation of the developers, Hubert Leach Ltd and Moody Homes Ltd. This was completed by the end of 1989 and altogether 2,579 coins were found, covering the period AD 193 to 263. The coins show the heads of a number of Roman emperors and members of their families. Perhaps the most interesting are those showing the head of Pacatian, nowadays a virtually unheard-of emperor who seized power for only a few months in AD 249. In that short time he had coins minted to help establish his authority, but to no avail as he was murdered by his own army. However, his name lives on in Stevenage in the modern road Pacatian Way and the nearby public house The Emperor's Head.

Of all the Roman remains in and around Stevenage, and notwithstanding the excitement of the treasure trove discovered in Chells, it is the Six Hills which are the most visible and solid reminder of the Roman occupation. Built around AD 100 close beside the road which was to become the Great North Road, they were burial mounds for important and wealthy Romans, possibly for a rich family which farmed the surrounding land.

Six Hills beside the main road into Stevenage. This drawing was made in July 1824 and emphasizes the way the hills appeared to dominate the surrounding countryside.

From the time they were built the Six Hills have been landmarks. Over the centuries they have become linked with Stevenage in the minds of travellers, who looked out for them as they approached the town on foot, on horseback, by stage-coach, train or car. Myths grew up about them, such as the story that the devil, digging pits in Whomerley Wood, threw six great spadefuls of earth over his shoulder, which landed in a line beside the road to form the Six Hills. In the nineteenth century people even forgot they were Roman and speculated that they were the tombs of Viking warriors. The final insult came when the new town was built and the route of the former Great North Road was changed, leaving the magnificent Six Hills stranded on an island, reduced from their former imposing status to mere preserved curiosities.

Despite all the evidence of a Roman presence in the Stevenage district, nothing at all is known about the people themselves. Life for both Romans and Britons, however, must have been dangerous and frightening at times. During the rebellion of the Iceni and the Trinovantes, led by Queen Boadicea in AD 61, great cruelties were carried out by both sides. The British queen led her armies to burn Colchester, London and St Albans, all near enough to have repercussions on Stevenage. Ultimately the Romans were victorious and remained to govern England for the following three hundred years, until invasion by Saxons and other continental tribes began and the Romans departed in 383.

CHAPTER TWO

Saxons, Danes and Normans

From the mid-fourth century Britain was invaded by a succession of different races, from the Picts and Irish in what is now Scotland to the Saxons, Angles and Jutes who eventually conquered England. After the Roman legions withdrew in 383, the way was clear for the newcomers to plunder their cities and villas, establish a different pattern of life and to introduce a new language which would eventually unite the whole country.

It was during the Saxon era that the name 'Stevenage' emerged to identify a village of wooden huts on the hill where St Nicholas' church now stands. Early variants of the name include 'Stithenace' and 'Stigenace' in the eleventh century, 'Stivenache', 'Styvenach' and 'Stiveneth' in the thirteenth century, 'Stivenhatch' in the fourteenth century and 'Stivenach' in the sixteenth century. The meaning of the name is generally accepted as 'At the stiff, or strong, oak' but some scholars argue for 'At the strong gate'.

The Saxon village of Stevenage may have been clustered round a wooden church on the hilltop, or it may have been a more scattered settlement of farmsteads on the rising ground above the Roman road below. There was security on the hill, whence it would be possible to keep a look-out for intruders and so repel attackers. Nearby the present St Nicholas' church is the Old Bury which may originally have been a wooden Saxon building. 'Bury', a term used extensively in Hertfordshire, is the word used for a manor-house. The presence of a bury indicates the existence of a sizeable community, which would need its own centre of justice and local government.

There were other settlements in the district; at Chells (Scelve or Escelvia), at Woolenwick and in Whomerley, or Humley, Wood, where a group of wooden houses, cattle sheds and barns was surrounded by a moat which protected it from marauders. The remains of this homestead moat can still be seen today.

Further evidence of Saxon occupation was found at Broadwater in

The church of St Nicholas, with the Old Bury beside it, marks the place where the Saxon village of Stigenace w first established.

1961 when Irene Traill, then Assistant Curator at Stevenage Museum, excavated a wooden hut in the garden of a house in Broadwater Crescent. She reported,

> The hut lay on sloping ground, high enough to command views over the surrounding countryside, but set below the brow of the hill as a protection from northerly winds. Below the hut flows the stream which rises in the centre of Stevenage and runs between the present-day Hertford Road and this end of Broadwater Crescent and then it flows into the River Beane.

Unfortunately we do not know whether this hut was part of a large settlement or just an isolated building. It is not even clear whether it was a dwelling, some kind of store, or an official meeting-place. It is tempting to believe that there was a substantial village here, if only because that 'small stream' gave its name not only to the immediate locality, but to the Hundred of Broadwater, a Saxon administrative district which included places such as Welwyn, Hatfield, Knebworth and Baldock. Originally composed of one hundred families, the Hundred was an early form of local government, being a sub-division of a shire and having its own court. In Hertfordshire some Hundreds were named after settlements still important today, such as Hertford. Others, for example Odsey, Cashio and Broadwater, were named after places now much diminished, or even vanished.

By the seventh century the Saxon invasion of Hertfordshire was complete and most of it became part of the great kingdom of Mercia.

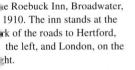

e Roebuck Inn, Broadwater, 1910. The inn stands at the rk of the roads to Hertford, the left, and London, on the ht.

Benington, now a picturesque village on the River Beane, was then an important Mercian stronghold and the scene of many an impressive gathering of nobles and soldiers.

It was during this period that the language of those other Germanic invaders, the Angles, came gradually to predominate as English. Interestingly, scholars now believe that most of Hertfordshire was still inhabited largely by the ancient British people whose ancestors had been here since before the Romans came, and that they continued to talk in an old Celtic language which was not unlike the Welsh tongue. The nearest river to Stevenage, the Beane, was still referred to by its old British name of Beneficcan (pronounced 'fitchen') well into the Middle Ages and the Lea has also retained its original British name, although now somewhat distorted. Probably it was not until the eighth or even the ninth century AD that most people in Hertfordshire had adopted the English language. Even then there were pockets of British speakers quite near to Stevenage, at Cumberlow Green, Walsworth and the villages now known as King's Walden and St Paul's Walden.

During the ninth century more invaders came, the Vikings or Danes. North and east Hertfordshire was the setting for some bitter fighting and historic events. There is no way of knowing to what extent the little

The Old Bury, 1982.

Saxon village of Stigenace was directly affected, but stirring deeds were taking place very near. At Benington, in the year 850, a Council of Mercians and West Saxons was held to discuss measures for opposing the Danish advance. At Hertford and Ware there were frequent battles between Saxon and Dane until King Alfred diverted the River Lea at Ware and inflicted a significant defeat on the Danes. In the Treaty of Wedmore in 878, it was agreed that the River Lea from the Thames to its source at Leagrave should form the boundary between Saxons to the west and Danes to the east. Stevenage would thus have been in Danish hands, but it was so near the boundary that it is likely that skirmishes continued in the district. The number of places known as Dane End also point to the possibility of changes to the boundary.

The next invasion came in 1066 when William of Normandy landed at Hastings, conquering both the Saxon King Harold and the remaining Danes. It was in Hertfordshire, at Berkhamsted Castle on Christmas Day, 1066, that William was acknowledged king by the English nobles and bishops. He swiftly set about establishing the feudal system of government and rewarded his Norman followers for their support by giving them land, including whole towns and villages. This resulted in some of them becoming extremely rich and powerful. One such baron was Peter de Valognes, who held land locally at Chells, Woolenwick and Box, as well as in other parts of

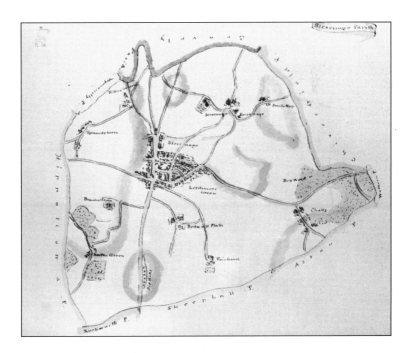

evenage parish, *c.* 1750.

the country. William also made him High Sheriff of the counties of Hertfordshire and Essex jointly, a slightly unusual arrangement.

Other Normans who held land in and around Stevenage included Bishop Odo of Bayeux, Robert Gernon, Geofrey de Bech and William de Ow. Stevenage itself, however, had been given by Edward the Confessor to the Abbey of St Peter at Westminster in about 1062 and William the Conqueror was content to confirm this. Domesday Book, that invaluable historical document which William intended should list every piece of land in the country, with details of its ownership, population and productivity, states that, 'The Abbot holds Stevenage himself'. The manor (the unit of land belonging to a lord) of Stevenage, as described in Domesday Book, comprised 8 hides (one hide equalled about 120 acres), land for 10 ploughs and included as tenants 16 villeins (tenant villagers), 8 bordars (the lowest-ranking villeins) and 4 serfs, plus their families. There may also have been others. Domesday Book also mentions Box, Chells (Scelve or Escelvia), Woolenwick (now Symonds Green) and Shephall (Escepehale), which was owned by the Abbot of St Albans.

CHAPTER THREE

The Middle Ages, *c.* 1135–1485

arly in the twelfth century, perhaps as early as the year 1100, a flint tower was built on to the wooden Saxon church of St Nicholas. The Norman kings William I and II had established an orderly society, but the reign of Henry I (1100–35) ended in confusion over the succession to the throne, which degenerated into civil war after King Stephen was crowned. To protect themselves from the depredations of mercenaries, communities throughout the country built strong church towers in which they could take refuge and the St Nicholas tower (which, of course, had no spire at that time) is part of this process. The narrow slit windows in the thick walls enabled the villagers crowded into the tower confines to shoot arrows at marauders without much fear of effective reprisal. The danger in these situations was of a siege developing, during which the villagers could be starved into submission.

In spite of frequent periods of lawlessness, it was at some time during the Middle Ages that the inhabitants of Stevenage took the step which was to alter the whole future history of their village. The majority of the community migrated down the hill and settled beside the old Roman road. This was a bold move which probably took place over a period of years, with the braver – or more mercenary – going first and the more cautious following later. The attraction was the trade to be had from passing travellers, who would pay for food, drink and lodging and in their turn brought goods for sale, news from the capital and perhaps entertainment from minstrels and jesters. There was, too, the added convenience of being near the road when transporting local produce to London as required by the lord of the manor, the Abbot of Westminster. A regular stream of traffic to and from London and the north, on foot, on horseback or in farm wagons, passed through Stevenage. Often travellers banded together for protection and companionship, as there was safety in numbers in those uncertain days.

The Bowling Green, *c.* 1910.
The Great North Road is on
the right and Hitchin Road on
the left.

One very important commodity was corn – wheat, barley and oats –
which was grown in abundance in the fertile fields of north-east
Hertfordshire. This type of farming had its centre at Ashwell, a
prosperous and important town in the early Middle Ages. Much of
the corn was transported to London by road as far as Hertford, where
it was transferred to boats and taken down the River Lea to the
capital. Some of it passed through Stevenage, increasingly so after
the development of an early 'new town' at Baldock, only a few miles
away. Built by the Knights Templars towards the end of the twelfth
century as a commercial centre, Baldock gradually eclipsed Ashwell,
but could never rival the long established market town of Hitchin as
the 'capital' of north Hertfordshire.

As well as traders, the road through Stevenage to St Albans in
medieval times would also see parties of pilgrims on their way to St
Albans, where the ornate shrine in the abbey was a focus for the
devout.

The number of surviving documents from the Middle Ages is
considerable and they help provide information about the
communities within the district now known as Stevenage. Many of
these documents relate to the ownership and value of land, and to
legal matters, including details of crime and punishment. The picture

such records paint is an incomplete one, but even so, a surprising amount is known about medieval Stevenage. Records show that within the boundaries of Stevenage parish there were several manors, usually owned by families who were not resident there. One was Homeleys, which probably took its name from the family of Ivo de Homeley or Homlie who is known to have held land in Stevenage in 1275. Today their memory is enshrined in the wood of the same name, pronounced 'Humley', or 'Humbly', but now spelled Whomerley.

Another manor which was to become closely associated with Homeleys through ownership of land, was Half Hyde. Little is known of its early history, but at the beginning of the fifteenth century it was held by John Chertsey of Broxbourne, whose family by that time had also acquired Homeleys. John Chertsey and his descendants were substantial landholders in Stevenage. In 1315, it is recorded, he held from the Abbot of Westminster the manor of Cannix, or Canwykes which, over a century later, had become known by his own name of Broxbourne. It was probably Cannix which was referred to as 'John de Broxbourn's manor of Stevenage' in 1308 when he was granted a licence to establish an oratory there. Oratories were small chapels, often reserved for private use only.

Yet another local manor, Bromesend, was acquired by the Chertsey family in the fifteenth century. Its name was probably taken from the family of Brome, one of whom, Roger atte Brome, is recorded as holding a messuage (house and garden) and half a virgate (about 15 acres) of land in the reign of Edward II. He was succeeded by Robert atte Brome, in the time of Edward III. There was also a lady, Anabill Brome, who had previously held 2 acres in Chalkdellfield.

The manor of Brooks, or Brokes or Brokys, took its name from the Brok family. Laurence de Brok, son of Adam de Brok, who died in about 1275, held 300 acres of land and a capital messuage (i.e. occupied by the owner of the property) from the Abbot of St Albans, 200 acres with a windmill from the Abbot of Westminster, 140 acres from Ivo de Homeley and 100 acres from Robert de Graveley. Some, or all, of these properties were probably known as Brooks.

The manor of Chells changed hands a number of times after the Norman Conquest. Roger le Strange owned it in 1295, but did not live there. It was let to the Pateshull family for many years, but by the end of the sixteenth century it belonged to the Boteler or Butler family. Approximately one hundred years later it was sold to Thomas Ashby, a London merchant.

Chells manor house, a timber framed, plaster-clad building. (Drawing, dated 1906, by Mr G. Aylott.)

Thus, at the time the township of Stevenage was establishing itself along the main road, there were also several manor-houses, each with its own dependent community in the neighbourhood. As well as these manors, there were the two small villages on the outskirts of Stevenage. Box, between Chells and Walkern, and Chesfield between Stevenage and Graveley, were both tiny even at the time of the Domesday survey. Box was then recorded as having a population of fourteen and there is evidence that it had its own church, almost certainly built of wood, in Saxon times. Chesfield was slightly larger and had its flint church dedicated to St Etheldreda. To the south of Stevenage lay the village of Shephall, also with its own church, dedicated to St Mary.

This time of development for Stevenage was also a time of transition for the social and commercial life of the country as a whole. During the twelfth century, the feudal system, whereby tenants did service for the lord of the manor by working on his land, transporting his produce to London, or carrying out some other work for him, gradually fell into disuse. By the end of the century it had become quite common for tenants to pay rent in money rather than service and increasingly farm work was being carried out by hired labour.

It is recorded that in Stevenage in 1308 only 33 acres were reaped by hired labourers and 293 acres were reaped by tenants as part of their service, although threshers were all hired. By 1338–9 the threshing, reaping, binding and hoeing were all being done by hired labourers. Wages for labourers varied throughout the country but Stevenage was probably about average, with hedgers and ditchers paid 2d. per day, ploughmen 6d. per acre and threshers 1d. per nine bushels. Rates were slightly different in John Chertsey's Broxbourne estate, 20 miles south-east, where labourers were paid 1d. per day, the man who drove the plough team of oxen was paid 1½d. per day and a wheelwright, a very skilled man, could earn up to 3d. per day.

Throughout Hertfordshire in the thirteenth and fourteenth centuries the emphasis was on arable farming. Cattle lost their value since murrain (an infectious disease) made them difficult and unprofitable to keep. For most households, such cows as they had supplied their domestic needs only. Also, meadowland in Hertfordshire was generally scarce and therefore expensive. It is thought that the average tenant farm covered about 12 acres of land. If the farmer wanted more he might be able to rent it, at 4d. per acre in Stevenage in 1275, but only 2d. per acre in Broxbourne in 1392. Meadowland remained steady at 2s. (10p) an acre in both places.

One of the most noticeable changes to the farming landscape in the thirteenth century was the introduction of large flocks of sheep and the subsequent importance of wool to the economy. The Chertsey family, with extensive lands in Broxbourne and Suffolk as well as Stevenage, amassed a substantial fortune from the woollen industry.

Although the majority of Stevenage's population made its living from the land, the late thirteenth century saw a greater concentration of dwellings and commerce along the main road. Trades such as innkeeping and blacksmithing grew up to serve the many travellers who passed through the area. There were also increasing opportunities for buying and selling, and vendors' booths set up as temporary shelters gradually became permanent and established the beginnings of the now familiar High Street, with rows of shops. The first of these was in what is now Middle Row.

In 1281 King Edward I granted the Abbot of Westminster, as lord of the manor, a royal charter entitling him to hold a fair at Stevenage on the vigil, feast and morrow of St John the Baptist – that is 23, 24 and 25 June – and to hold a market on Mondays. In later years the dates and frequency of fairs and markets were revised on several occasions, but the original charter of 1281 was a significant point in the growth of Stevenage as a town. Medieval fairs, although colourful and entertaining, were first and foremost important trading opportunities. They not only provided outlets for the sale of all kinds

Middle Row, in the centre of the High Street, was the place where medieval traders set up their booths, which eventually became permanent shops.

of goods, but they were also used for hiring labour and on other business transactions. The existence of a fair gave a town status and attracted people with money to spend. It also, of course, provided extra income, by way of fees, to the lord of the manor.

Whether the fairs and markets attracted them, or whether their influence persuaded the king to grant the charter, will perhaps never be known, but it is clear that during the Middle Ages a number of wealthy London merchants bought land in Stevenage. As it grew into a town, so Stevenage began to acquire the trappings of urban life. Law enforcement was a necessity and this was carried out in England by a system of parish constables. Annually each parish appointed one of its ratepayers to the unpaid office of constable, to keep the peace and maintain law and order. This system worked well for many years, although the 'unpaid' aspect of the work varied. Some constables charged a fee for every prisoner brought to court; other citizens, shrinking from taking their turn as constable, paid someone else to do it for them. No doubt there were also other ways of reimbursing a constable.

In 1310 Stevenage had its own prison and in that year Andrew Baron, about whom nothing is known except that he was accused of larceny, fled to St Nicholas' church for sanctuary. He was seized by 'certain malefactors' who dragged him off to the prison, but fortunately for him the Justices of the Peace ordered that he be released and taken back to the church. There is no record of the rest of the story.

During the thirteenth and early fourteenth centuries the Abbot of Westminster held five courts a year for the people of Stevenage. Ways of punishing offenders included placing them in a pillory, for passers-by to hurl refuse at them, or ducking them in a pond. Fines could also be imposed, perhaps less degrading for the offender and certainly profitable to the lord of the manor. This punishment was inflicted on John Hamond in 1377, for 'carrying away corn from the lord's field.' Apart from offences such as theft, trespass or assault, the manor court also had responsibility for enforcing the upkeep of roads, the trimming of hedges and other essential duties of civilized life.

In 1315 the Abbot of Westminster employed the services of twelve citizens to make a survey of land and property ownership in Stevenage. The twelve – William de Chelse, Roger Trot, Roger atte Uppehende, John Shush or Sish, Thomas atte Grave, Robert atte Cherch, Richard Feveral, John Couppere, Eustace atte Dane, Roger le Rene, John atte Herne and Roger atte Grave – were sworn to give an honest account. They produced detailed lists of property with names of occupiers, the amount of rent each paid and information about obligations due from tenant to lord of the manor. For example, Annabel Geffray was required to make a number of payments in kind, including two hens worth 1½d. each, every Christmas.

Following the building of its flint tower, St Nicholas' church was continually extended and altered. During the thirteenth century it was almost completely rebuilt, except for the tower. In about 1330 the present chancel was built and the aisles widened, and at some time during the fourteenth century the roof was pitched higher than at present, to enclose the door from the tower. In common with other medieval churches, the interior was brilliant with wall paintings, stained glass and possibly tapestry hangings and a decorated roof. There would be missals (service books) in illuminated manuscript for the clergy while for the illiterate peasants there would be much to learn from the colourful murals.

Early schools often took place in churches, sometimes in the church porch and although it is possible that this occurred at St Nicholas' there is also evidence of the existence of a school elsewhere in Stevenage in 1312. At Michaelmas (30 September) that year, the annual report of the reeve (the bailiff or steward) of Stevenage to the lord of the manor, the Abbot of Westminster, included the following statement of account:

> For the board of William, son of Richard le Rous, being in the schools of Stevenage from the Feast of St Mark the Evangelist to St Michael's day, 22 weeks and 3 days, 18/8 that is to say 10d a week. For 3 yards of blue cloth bought for a tunic and a hood for the use of the same, 3/9. For the making of the same, with a pair of sleeves of the robe of the same, 8d. For 2 caps bought for the use of the same, 3/8. For shirts bought for the use of the same, 2/-. For one pair of linen cloths bought for the use of the same, 12d. For one pair of stockings and 2 pairs of shoes bought for the use of the same, 20d.

Where the school (or schools) was located is not certain, but there is a strong tradition that it was on land adjacent to the Bury Mead, which belonged to the church. It is not impossible that it was the forerunner of the Grammar School, endowed two centuries later by the Revd Thomas Alleyne. There existed in Stevenage in the Middle Ages a guild, or brotherhood, dedicated to the Holy Trinity. Although there are many records of bequests made to it and it maintained a guild priest, there is no evidence that the priest was also a schoolmaster, as often happened elsewhere. However, there is a strong possibility that the guild had some connection with the medieval school.

The growth of trade, the expansion of the population, the spread of culture and learning which were occurring in medieval Stevenage were violently disrupted by the horrors of the Black Death, the name given to the great plague epidemics of 1350 and 1361. From the first outbreaks in 1348, in London, the plague spread swiftly along the major roads, reaching Stevenage in 1349. It is not known how many people died but, in common with the rest of the country, Hertfordshire towns and villages had their populations depleted.

The long-term effects of the Black Death were considerable. One immediate result was that the cost of hired labour, for example, at harvest time, increased often to double the previous rate. In Ashwell, in 1352, men could charge 10d. for reaping 1 acre of wheat, as against the 5d. laid down by the Statute of Labourers in 1351. Another result was the number of villeins who left their homes illegally, without paying the 'chevage' due to the lord of the manor for the right to do so. They then sought employment in towns, as craftsmen or domestic servants, leaving behind a countryside which was rapidly becoming depopulated and unproductive. The manor court records of Stevenage, unlike those of many Hertfordshire towns, do not contain records of these 'fugitives' as they were called. It may be that Stevenage, as an established market town, was attracting people, rather than losing them.

The Black Death severely afflicted the neighbouring communities of Box and Chesfield, which became 'deserted villages' and never recovered from losses among their already tiny populations. Chesfield struggled on with its own priest until 1445 when the living was united with that of Graveley, but Box was even smaller and succumbed altogether, its wooden church, which it had shared with Chells, being left to decay.

The latter part of the fourteenth century was a time of discontent among the common people because of the high taxes they were required to pay to help fund crusades to the Holy Land. In 1377 the parliament of King Richard II imposed its infamous poll-tax and rashly followed it in 1380 with an additional graduated poll-tax. This sparked off the Peasants' Revolt of 1381, led by Wat Tyler. Hertfordshire was at the centre of some of the fiercest rebellion, as its taxes were particularly heavy. During the revolt, the men of Shephall obtained a charter from the Abbot of St Albans, their lord of the manor, granting them a number of rights including common

16

pasture, rights of way, fishing, chase, and so on, as well as the right of self-government. Stevenage, whose lord of the manor was in London, did not, apparently, achieve any similar concessions. However, those of Shephall proved to be short-lived, as the king himself soon arrived in St Albans with powerful forces and revoked the charters which the rebels had won.

Nor were the years ahead any more peaceful. When Henry IV came to the throne in 1399 there were rebellions by the rich and powerful barons who owned so much land throughout the country. In the following century the Wars of the Roses brought death and destruction to many. Hertfordshire was the scene of much fighting, including the Battle of St Albans in 1455, which signalled the start of the Wars of the Roses, and the important Battle of Barnet in 1471. As well as these famous battles there were other skirmishes in Hertfordshire and the county's roads saw many a company of soldiers march by. No doubt a fair number came through Stevenage, perhaps pausing for food and rest and often giving the residents cause to breathe a sigh of relief when they left.

Almshouses in Church Lane, bequeathed to the town by rector Stephen Hellard in 1506. The building on the right housed the public slipper baths in the early part of the twentieth century.

In 1472 Stephen Hellard became Rector of Stevenage and remained until his death in 1506. In his will he directed that a messuage to be called All Christian Souls' House, which he had built in Dead Lane (later called Back Lane and now Church Lane), should be inhabited rent free by three poor people, who should pray for his soul daily. He also left to his trustees 7 acres of land called Gleviscroft, a pightle (small piece) of land adjoining and a piece of ground in Churchfield, the rent from which was to be used to maintain the property and to help support the tenants.

A brass memorial to Stephen Hellard, showing him dressed as a priest in his vestments, exists in St Nicholas' church, where he was buried. As there is no date of death on the brass, it is assumed that it was designed and made during his lifetime, perhaps by Hellard himself, or by his family or parishioners.

CHAPTER FOUR

Tudors and Stuarts

B y the beginning of the sixteenth century, the roadside town of Stevenage extended from a little way north of the Bowling Green to the junction of Sish Lane with the High Street; in other words, it approximated very closely to what is now the High Street. Behind the road, on either side, stretched open countryside thinly populated by outlying farms and hamlets, in much the same locations as in Roman, ancient British or even prehistoric times.

Of the outlying manors, Brooks was the subject of a family feud at the beginning of the sixteenth century, following the death of its

The interior of 9A Middle Row, showing detail of structural beams and braces. This building was the Buckingham Palace public house during the nineteenth and early twentieth centuries.

owner, Edmund Node. His widow, Joan, conferred the inheritance to her second son, William, on condition that he made an estate to his elder brother, also called William. The younger son refused to comply and between 1493 and 1500 his mother brought a lawsuit against him. It is not clear what the outcome was, since in 1521 a William Nodes was in possession of Brooks and seems to have been succeeded by another William, who sold the manor in 1564 to Robert Ivory.

The neighbouring manor of Broxbournes or Cannix had, in about 1509, been acquired for 40s. by William Canwyke from his mother, Petronilla. In 1510 it belonged to Samuel and Clemence Canwyke and subsequently passed to William Lytton of Knebworth.

The Lytton family seemed at this period to be taking every opportunity of acquiring land in the locality. The manor of Half Hyde, which had previously belonged to the Chertseys, was owned in the early sixteenth century by Matthew Ward and his wife, Alice. In 1553 they sold the property to John, Lord Mordaunt, who was succeeded in 1561 by his son, John. The second John's son, Lewis, inherited Half Hyde in 1571 and sold it in 1601 to Rowland Lytton and Sir Henry Wallop, the latter subsequently conveying his share of the property to Rowland Lytton in 1610.

Homeleys, which had also belonged to the Chertsey family, followed the same course as Half Hyde and came into the hands of the Lyttons. Bromesend, another Stevenage manor which had belonged to the wealthy Chertsey family, was acquired by the Lyttons at the same time.

The other two manors of which some history is known, Chells and Box, were both in the possession of John Norreys at the beginning of the sixteenth century. In 1526 Boxbury was sold to Philip Boteler and at about the same time Chells was also conveyed to the Botelers.

As for the town of Stevenage, it remained the property of the Abbot of Westminster. The Church at this period of history was rich and powerful, with abbeys such as Westminster employing large numbers of people and owning vast acreages of land. Most had also acquired treasures of silver, gold, or precious stones and the much revered bones of saints. During the Middle Ages the Church had been at the centre of life and most people accepted its teachings unquestioningly. The fifteenth century was to see a series of dramatic challenges to established religious tradition. The local church was the source of practical as well as spiritual comfort, the priest often being given responsibility for administering charities to feed, clothe or house the poor. Some priests, such as Stephen Hellard, left money themselves for this purpose.

Baker Street, 1987. The wooden hut on the left was used during the mid-twentieth century by the Salvation Army

It was common practice for people making their wills at this time to begin with a standard form of words, including a dedication to God and his saints. After the Reformation mention of the saints was normally omitted, except by a few brave Roman Catholics who insisted on retaining these words. Thus the preliminary wording in surviving sixteenth- and seventeenth-century wills can give a clue to the religious tendencies of the deceased. Most wills were written out by scribes, formally witnessed and signed by the testator, sometimes with a cross if he or she could not write.

The will of Richard Barfoyte, dated 20 June 1529, shows the importance of the traditions of the Catholic Church:

> I Richard Barfoyte of the town and parish of Stevenage in the county of Hertford and in the Diocese of Lincoln, whole of mind and memory but sick in body make my last will and testament after this form and manner following; First I bequeath my soul to God Almighty, to Our Lady Saint Mary and to all the company of heaven, my body, to be buried in the churchyard of St Nicholas of the said Stevenage . . .

He went on to leave 4d. for the high altar at St Nicholas' church, 2d. to the mother church, or cathedral of Lincoln, a field at 'Nicolles Grene' to his son, Nicholas, and 3 acres of arable land in Lady Hill to his son, Robert. The remainder of his property went to his wife, Elisabeth.

Richard Barfoyte died shortly before the full force of the Reformation struck Britain. In 1531 King Henry VIII declared himself Supreme Head of the English Church, in defiance of the Pope's authority, although for the time being England had not yet officially embraced the teachings of the Protestants. Walter Bedwell, a Stevenage man of some wealth, who died in 1536, was still using the traditional formula of dedicating his soul 'to Almighty God and to Our Lady Saint Mary and to all the holy company in heaven.' Among several bequests to St Nicholas' church was 4d. for 'Our Lady's light'.

Apparently a widower with young children, Walter was anxious to make adequate provision for his family. As was usual, he left his house and land to his eldest son, John, but because John was a minor, Walter made his daughter, Katherine, guardian of the family until the eldest son came of age. Among her duties, Katherine was charged to 'honestly find the said John meat and drink and all other apparel to him belonging till he be able to find himself and to earn his living.' Walter's youngest child he put in the care of his daughter, Alice, apparently a married woman, to whom he left a quantity of goods including:

my wife's best gown, a coverlet next the best, a mattress with the worst bolster and the best pillow . . . Also a violet gown lined with black cotton, also a kettle next the best, a little brass pot, 2 pewter pots, 2 pewter platters, a candlestick next the best, the best chafing dish and a latten [copper alloy] basin.

To his daughter, Katherine, he left money, '2 beasts, 2 hogs and all the residue of my moveable goods . . . '.

Fully aware of the hazards of sixteenth-century life, Walter also provided for the eventuality that one or both of his sons might not reach the age of majority. If the worst happened, 'as God forbid', then he left instructions for part of his estate to be divided between his daughters, Katherine and Alice, and some money 'to be given to an honest priest to pray for my soul, my wife's soul and all Christian souls.'

During the tumultuous and often distressing times following Henry VIII's decision in 1530 to dissolve the English monasteries, no doubt Stevenage, in its roadside location, heard all kinds of conflicting opinions from travellers. The rector in 1530 was almost certainly the Revd Thomas Offley, about whom there is little surviving information. However, in Fox's *Book of Martyrs*, which recounts in gruesome detail the histories and sufferings of the English Protestants who were put to death for their beliefs, there is an interesting statement about Offley's successor, the Revd Thomas Alleyne. It refers to a martyr by the name of Bilney who, in 1531, was burnt to death at Norwich. One of his friends, who witnessed the horrible proceedings, was apparently Thomas Alleyne, the implication being that he had Protestant sympathies. In 1536, Henry VIII began to close down the monasteries, taking their buildings, land and possessions and selling them to the highest bidder, or sometimes giving them as rewards for loyal service. The nearest great monastery to Stevenage was St Albans and by coincidence the abbot there in 1537 was Richard Stevenage, later known as Richard Boreman. In 1539, following the dissolution of the abbey, he was given a pension of £266 13s. 4d., a substantial sum for those days. Richard Stevenage was next heard of in 1551, when he was authorized to set up a grammar school at St Albans.

The Abbey of Westminster, which owned the town of Stevenage, was not dissolved until 1539–40, when the monastery and its possessions were given up to the king. By the end of 1540 a new bishopric of Westminster had been established, endowed with the lands which had formerly belonged to the monastery, including, of course, Stevenage. There is no way of telling what effect, if any, these changes had on the people of Stevenage. As far as their relationship with their own parish church of St Nicholas is concerned, presumably church services took on a Protestant form, but otherwise life seems to have continued much as before, with the rector as the leading figure in the town.

At Box, the little church which was shared with Chells was in a state of decay by 1530. The few remaining dwellers in these two tiny hamlets now had to journey either to Walkern or Stevenage to attend church. Walkern is the more likely choice, as the history of Box has since been recorded with that of Walkern. The sixteenth-century inhabitants of these rural outposts might well look to Walkern as being not only nearer, but equally as important as Stevenage, having within its boundaries the remains of a twelfth-century castle built by Hamo de St Clare, and its ancient church of St Mary, one of the oldest in Hertfordshire, of pre-Norman origin.

In the secular world, law and order were always matters of great importance. In 1542 orders came from Westminster that the stocks (into which wrong-doers were fixed while passers-by threw rubbish at them) must be repaired and the ducking-stool and pillory, which had both been allowed to decay, must be replaced.

Much information about the lives of ordinary people is available from their wills. Edward Ansell, who died in 1543, gave his occupation in his will as labourer – that is, a worker on a farm – but the will also makes clear that he had a shop, as he left to his son, Thomas, 'my whole shop and all things pertaining thereto.' One of the witnesses to the will was Roger Butte, the Brotherhood priest.

The following year, 1544, John Anderson, haberdasher, died. His will gives a summary of life in the sixteenth century. After the usual preamble, he willed:

> I bequeath to Sir Roger Butte ['Sir' indicates a priest] a pair of flaxen sheets. I will to Sir William Dyer, being parish priest, a pair of flaxen sheets. I bequeath to Nicholas Sawndere my marble [patterned] coat. I bequeath to every one of my Godchildren 6d. I bequeath to John Boswell a pewter platter and a saucer . . . I bequeath to Margaret that dwelled with me 2 saucers and a candlestick. I will to Marion Slater a ewe and a lamb. I will to John Gynne of the Falcon, the elder, 12d. [The Falcon Inn stood in the High Street, close beside the Red Lion] . . . I will to a wife of Benington that was called Joan Baker when she was single 12d [and] to Mother Walker of Aston, 12d . . .

I bequeath to everyone of my children, if it please God that they do live, 20/-. I bequeath unto my wife if it please God to give her life, that after my debts paid and legacies before given and bequeathed performed, the residue of all my goods, corn and chattels. And if it shall happen my said wife to die and also all my children this plague time without issues of their bodies lawfully begotten, that then I will and bequeath the residue of all my goods, corn, chattels and household stuff, debts [owed to me] and ready money . . . as hereafter is declared;

First I will that all my lands, tenements with all and singular their appurtenances . . . to be sold by Master Alleyne, now Parson of Stevenage, unto whom I have declared my secret mind . . . and the money thereof . . . to be given and distributed among poor people of the inhabitants of the said town of Stevenage, £6..13s..4d.

It is clear from John Anderson's will that plague was rife in the district in the mid-sixteenth century. It was even worse in London, so much so that King Henry VIII often stayed in Hertfordshire to avoid it. His children, Princess Mary, Princess Elizabeth and Prince Edward were also put into safekeeping in Hertfordshire; first at Hunsdon, and then at Hatfield, in the care of the Countess of Salisbury. There were other links with royalty and government closer to Stevenage, at Knebworth. There had been a castle at Knebworth from the time of the Norman Conquest and during the reign of Edward I it had belonged to one of the royal princes. In the sixteenth century it was bought by Sir Robert Lytton, a member of Henry VIII's Privy Council.

In 1547 King Henry VIII died and was succeeded by his son, the young and sickly Edward VI, who was to live for only six more years. It was during his brief reign that England became a Protestant country, renouncing the Roman Catholic faith. The buying and selling of former monastic property continued.

In 1553 the young king died and was succeeded by his half-sister, Mary. At once she set about re-establishing Roman Catholicism and persecuting Protestant adherents, just as in the previous reign Catholics had been persecuted. Hertfordshire people generally seem to have supported the Protestant faith and a number who refused to renounce it were put to death as martyrs in Mary's reign. Probably the majority kept quiet and conformed to the prevailing religion in order to protect themselves from punishment, torture or death. Certainly Richard Boreman is known to have handed St Albans

Abbey over to Queen Mary in 1556. No doubt she wished to re-found the monastery and Boreman preferred to lose his property rather than his life. There is no surviving information about how these matters affected Stevenage, but it is certain that travellers would bring news about the burning of heretics as they paused for refreshment at the High Street inns. In 1550 the manor of Stevenage had changed hands. It had been given by Edward VI to the newly created Bishopric of London, under Bishop Ridley. In 1554 Mary confirmed this arrangement, although, of course, the religion of the Church was now Roman Catholic. Bishop Ridley was one of those who refused to accept this and he was burnt at the stake in Oxford.

Although the question of religious belief may seem to have dominated life in the sixteenth century, there were other, more worldly matters to be attended to, such as travel and the state of the roads. One Act of Parliament which became law in Mary's reign and was to continue in force for almost three hundred years was the Highways Act of 1555, which required parishioners to give four days' unpaid service annually (later increased to six days) to mend the roads in that parish and to provide their own horses and carts for that purpose. Universally unpopular, the Act was to place a

Southend Farm, 1975.

particularly heavy burden on places such as Stevenage and even more on little Graveley, which were forced to assume responsibility for main roads to London.

The year 1558 was an historic one for Stevenage. The Brotherhood House, with 6 acres of land belonging to it 'late of the Fraternity of the Holy Trinity', was granted to Sir George Howarde 'in consideration of his service' by the queen. This seems to have marked the end of the Brotherhood of the Holy Trinity and it is frustrating not to know more. It seems particularly odd that it should be during a Catholic queen's reign that the property of a traditional Catholic institution should be disposed of.

In some towns it was the practice for the Brotherhood priest to take on the role of schoolmaster. Although no evidence has been found that this happened in Stevenage, it is possible that there is some significance in the fact that the sale of the Brotherhood House occurred in the same year as the death of the Revd Thomas Alleyne, who bequeathed land to the Master, Fellows and Scholars of Trinity College, Cambridge, part of the income from which they were to use to found and maintain three free grammar schools, one at Uttoxeter, one at Stone and one at Stevenage.

Alleyne's Grammar School was opened in a building beside the Bury Mead, opposite the Bowling Green at the top of the High Street. Although there is no direct evidence that the new school was established on the site of the already existing Petits' School, it is now considered very likely as, at this time, it was rare for a completely new school to be set up where none had previously existed.

Thomas Alleyne left detailed instructions about the running of his schools, including 'the learning of good authors and praying for me their founder morning and evening.' In the Catholic tradition he left money for masses to be said for his soul. An annual sum of £5 6s. 8d. was also left, to be divided equally among four poor old men of

Alleyne's School House. (Watercolour sketch by H.G. Oldfield, 1800.)

Stevenage 'to pray to Almighty God for the weal of my soul.' This contrasts interestingly with other indications that Alleyne had Protestant sympathies, but perhaps in those dangerous and troubled times the business of keeping alive and free from persecution by either party was a major achievement.

On 17 November 1558 Queen Mary died and was succeeded by her half-sister, the Protestant Elizabeth, who was at Hatfield House when the news came that she was queen. She continued to visit Hertfordshire frequently throughout her reign, partly because the county offered a convenient rural sanctuary from the periodic outbreaks of plague in the capital and partly because of the loyalty of a number of the nobility with estates in Hertfordshire. Among these were the Lyttons of Knebworth, where Elizabeth stayed on at least one occasion. During her reign Sir Rowland Lytton was Lord Lieutenant of Hertfordshire and Essex.

The religious discord of her predecessors' days was to a large extent eliminated by Elizabeth's compromises, but towards the end of her reign there was a widespread fear of Roman Catholicism, due largely to the threat of a Spanish invasion. In 1588, the year of the Spanish Armada, the queen stayed at Knebworth. Many Hertfordshire men became soldiers of the queen, some as members of her own bodyguard. When the Armada was sighted in the English Channel a chain of beacons was lit throughout the country, the nearest to Stevenage being at Graveley, the next at Royston Heath.

As Stevenage prospered during Elizabeth's reign, so too did neighbouring Shephall. One indication of this was the number of people liable for taxation, which increased from two to six. Local wills of this period too give some idea of the life of late sixteenth-century Stevenage and the material wealth some now owned. Edmund Cuckowe, husbandman [farmer] made a detailed will, dated 4 August 1581, which featured an extensive list of household goods and farm stock, including:

> one tinker's kettle of 2 gallons measure by estimation
> one brass pot with the pothooks, 3 gallons by estimation
> one malt quern
> one ashen milk bowl
> one woollen wheel, with 2 elm joined stools
> one spit
> 2 andirons
> one salt cellar
> pewter dishes with saucers
> one great coffer 'standing in mine own chamber'.

To his maidservant, Alice Porter, he left the 'bedstead and all furniture and bedding wherein she lieth, the pair of sheets being herein comprehended.' His best black cloth jerkin he left to Edmunde Cooke, tailor of Stevenage. His son, John Cuckowe, inherited the bulk of his goods and estate. His beehives, clearly very valuable, received special mention:

> I will and bequeath to John Cuckowe my son and Alice Thurbye the daughter of Thomas Thurbye, all my hives of bees and bees' stools, to be equally divided between them at the discretion of two honest men, the one to be chosen by my son John Cuckowe and the other by Alice Thurbye and her friends.

The other invaluable documents which shed light on past ages are the records of court cases, such as those for the Hertford Assizes and the St Albans Assizes. A due proportion of Stevenage people feature in these, as is only to be expected of a sizeable market town.

At the Hertford Assize Court on 4 March 1573, John Harrison of Stevenage, a labourer, was found guilty of stealing from Affabell Battell, at Lannock (near Weston) a shirt, three table napkins, two kerchiefs and a shirtband. Theft on a larger scale occurred on 2 December 1584 when Henry Tyghton, John Howe, and William Johnson, all labourers of Stevenage, broke into the house of Edward Cooke at Stevenage, stealing 40 yards of woollen cloth worth £7, belonging to Cooke, and a buckskin doublet worth 13s. 4d. belonging to Robert Norris. On the same day they broke into another Stevenage house, that of Thomas Pynnock, and stole fifteen pairs of shoes worth 22s. and a butt of leather worth 9d.

Thefts of clothes and materials occurred frequently, as did sheep-stealing. On 12 July 1591 Richard Tyday, labourer of Stevenage, confessed at Hertford Assizes that he had stolen a sheep and a lamb worth 5s. from John Lylly, a sheep worth 5s. and a sheep and lamb worth 6s. from William Broke. All the thefts took place at Letchworth. Tyday was sentenced to hang.

Other court cases, such as that on 3 March 1598, were concerned with the regulation of trades. On this occasion Thomas Robinson, Cuthbert Kympton, Richard Kichyn, Henry Gynn, George Gynn and George Nodes, all bakers of Stevenage, were accused of unlawfully exercising the trade of baker without having served the seven years' apprenticeship stipulated by statute. At the St Albans Assizes on 23 July 1601, a Grand Jury heard the case of 'such persons as have made starch within the county of Hertfordshire contrary to Her

Majesty's proclamation.' Among the accused was William Mashe, yeoman of Stevenage.

Queen Elizabeth I died on 24 March 1603 and the Scottish King James VI became James I of England, thus uniting the two countries under one crown. What the people of Stevenage thought about this historic event is not known. Probably, in common with many of their countrymen, they were more concerned with the increasing poverty which afflicted so many, following several years of poor harvests. The Poor Law of 1601 established the office of Overseer of the Poor and empowered parishes to levy a rate (tax) to cover the cost. Subsequent amendments to the Act allowed for the setting up of 'workhouses' and made other arrangements to attempt to deal with poverty and homelessness.

James I often visited Hertfordshire, sometimes staying at Royston. However, since he would normally travel there along Ermine Street (the old North Road, now A10), it is probable that most of the inhabitants of Stevenage would be unaware that their king was so near. Of more pressing local interest would be the publication in 1614 of a list of thirty-four duties of parish constables, including the suppression of drunkenness and of Popish recusants (i.e. Roman Catholics), dealing with rogues and beggars and checking weights and measures. There were Head, or Chief, Constables to superintend the constables of a group of parishes and one Chief Constable to each Hundred. Records of the names of some Stevenage constables have survived, such as William Greene, who attended the Hertford Assizes on 15 July 1624.

The Lyttons of Knebworth continued to extend their landholdings in Stevenage. In 1601 Sir Rowland Lytton bought a share in the manor of Half Hyde and in 1610 was able to complete his purchase of the entire estate, which by then included Homeleys and Bromesend as well. Cannix, after some changes of ownership, eventually ended up in Lytton hands too. In 1616 William Lytton was granted free warren in Half Hyde, Homeleys and Bromesend. This meant that he was entitled to hunt hares, rabbits and game in the woodland, a right normally preserved for the king himself.

As befitted their position in society, the Lyttons played their part in helping to uphold the rule of law. Sir Rowland Lytton was a Justice of the Peace and as such took his turn to preside at local courts. For example, at the Assizes at Hertford on 2 December 1607, Sir Rowland heard the case against William Hooke, or Smyth, and Thomas Rochell, both labourers of Stevenage, who were accused of stealing a white horse valued at £4 and a sorrel gelding valued at £5 from Richard Boughton, at Stevenage. Richard Boughton and John Nodes, a Stevenage innkeeper, gave evidence against the accused. Rochell was acquitted but Hooke was found guilty and sentenced to hang.

Punishments varied considerably and it can only be assumed that magistrates and judges took into account information about the accused which has not been recorded. In 1622 Thomas Hodgkin, labourer of Stevenage, was found guilty of breaking into the house of Griffin Lewis at Stevenage and stealing a pair of stockings worth 6d. and a hat worth 4d., for which crime he was whipped. Given the customs of the time, this seems a reasonable punishment. More difficult to understand is the fate of Joseph Feild, a Graveley blacksmith who, on 10 March 1615, was accused of stealing a hatchet worth 6d. from Richard Hunt. He was found not guilty, but 'sent to the House of Correction'. On the other hand, Joan Hall, wife of John Hall of Stevenage, who was found guilty in 1603 of stealing two gowns worth 20s., two hats worth 10s. and a petticoat worth 5s. from Thomas Chapman, was remanded because she was pregnant. For serious crimes a Grand Jury was summoned; Stevenage men who served on it included Edward Kent (gentleman), Edward Fysh (gentleman), George Nodes of Shephall (gentleman), and William Potter of Bedwell, Stevenage.

Fairs and markets continued to be important to the prosperity of Stevenage. In 1624 King James granted the Bishop of London, as lord of the manor, three fairs to be held in Stevenage on Ascension Day, St Swithin's Day (15 July) and the following Friday. The market-day was altered to Friday.

In 1625 King James died, to be succeeded by his son, Charles, whose belief in the divine right of kings to rule without parliament, together with his imposition of the infamous Ship Tax and his religious views, clashed with the ideas of the increasingly vocal Puritans and Parliamentarians. Almost inevitably, the country drifted towards civil war, which finally erupted in 1642. Hertfordshire and East Anglia were generally supportive of the Parliamentarian cause and its leader, Oliver Cromwell. However, the crude antics of those Roundheads who desecrated churches, smashing stained glass, rood screens and altar rails and defacing murals, were viewed with disgust by many. Clergy who in any way opposed the Puritans had their livings sequestrated. Stevenage is not listed as one of the parishes where this happened, which could mean that the clergy were favourable to Puritanism, or that they prudently kept quiet. In 1649 the lands belonging to the Bishopric of London were sold in accordance with government policy and a Thomas Ayres bought the manor of Stevenage.

During the Civil War, Stevenage must have seen many troops passing through the town and no doubt some Stevenage men became soldiers for a time. Probably the majority of people, as in every war, just wished for an end to hostilities, to be rid of the plundering soldiers and to have the chance to live an ordered, peaceful life. Such was the confused state of the country in 1643–4 that Assize Courts had to be abandoned, and it became very difficult for the local authorities to maintain the rule of law. News of the war was circulated by means of newsletters and pamphlets which were delivered every morning from London by mounted newsmen who stopped at shire halls, Eleanor crosses or the crossroads of towns, announcing their approach by blowing a horn. The probable stopping place at Stevenage was the Bowling Green, where the road forked, a natural meeting-place for the townspeople.

Although most of Hertfordshire apparently supported the Parliamentarians, there were pockets of royalist support to the king in Hertford and Ware and at Hadham, where the royalist Lord Capel lived. Lord Salisbury of Hatfield decided to support Cromwell, as did Sir William Lytton, who entertained leading Parliamentarians at Knebworth, including John Hampden, and John Pym, whose verbal attacks on the king did much to start the Civil War.

In April 1646 King Charles, under siege at Oxford, disguised himself as a servant to his own chaplain and made his escape, travelling through Harrow, Stanmore, Edgware and St Albans to Wheathampstead, where he spent the night of 27 April. The next day he continued on the old road to Stevenage, then on to Baldock and Royston, through Cambridgeshire to Downham. The following year, this time in captivity, the king again passed through Stevenage on his way from Newmarket to Hatfield House. Although strongly Puritan, many Hertfordshire towns welcomed the king – Baldock was one place where the people were prepared to demonstrate their loyalty to him – and his progress was regal rather than that of a prisoner.

As the war dragged on, revulsion against the pillaging soldiers, not to mention the taxes levied to pay for the war, caused many people, even in counties like Hertfordshire where support for Cromwell was strong, to have regrets about the course of events. When the king was executed in 1649 there was a reaction against the Puritans in some places, including Puritan Royston, where soldiers were attacked 'in revenge for the blood of the late king.'

For the eleven years from 1649 England was a republic; the

monarchy, the House of Lords and the Anglican Church were all abolished, along with the traditional celebration of Christmas. Whatever mixed feelings the populace might have had about the outcome, once the war was over life gradually became settled and orderly again. Perennial problems reasserted themselves, such as the difficulty of keeping the roads in good condition. In 1658 there was a complaint that 'the common highway in Baldock leading from Stevenage to Biggleswade is in great decay and that the inhabitants of Baldock ought to repair the same.' Pedestrians suffered too. In 1660 Edward Spicer, late of Stevenage, 'did hedge up and stop 2 foot of the footpath in the common highway leading from Stevenage to the church of Stevenage.'

Oliver Cromwell, Lord Protector of England, died in 1658 and was succeeded to the title by his son, Richard, who was unequal to the task and abdicated on 24 May 1659, thereafter spending his life in peaceful anonymity in Cheshunt, Hertfordshire. After a year of parliamentary government, England was in a state of confusion, with quarrels among senior military commanders and the army in disarray. The fear of anarchy and public disorder prompted orders such as this for the raising of militia:

> To the constable of Stevenages, or either of them! You are upon sight hereof to give notice to the persons whose names are underwritten of the several charges the Commissioners for the Militia of this County have charged them with, towards the raising of a regiment of foot soldiers and arms, which soldiers and arms are hereby required forthwith to provide and have complete and in readiness to appear at an hour's warning: that is to say every musketeer with his musket, sword belt, bandoliers [broad leather belt for carrying ammunition] and knapsack. Hereof fail not. . . . This is done by a full consent of our townsmen. Robert Smith and Peter Lankhorn, Constables.

The order to the Stevenage constables was dated 1 May 1660. Five days later, on 5 May, Charles II was proclaimed king.

The monarchy was restored and with it many of the institutions abolished by the previous regime. The Bishopric of London was re-established and resumed ownership of the manor of Stevenage.

One of the men named in the militia list was Richard Bococke, who was required to supply one musket. He was the landlord of the Swan Inn, opposite the Bowling Green, a Stevenage hostelry well known to travellers. One of the Swan's most famous visitors was the diarist Samuel Pepys, who stayed there several times. He travelled frequently, on horseback or by coach, between London and his parents' home in Brampton, Huntingdonshire. His diary entry for 23 September 1661 states:

> We took horse and got early to Baldwick, where there was a fair, and we put in and eat a mouthful of pork, which they made us pay 14d for, which vexed us much. And so away to Stevenage and stayed 'till a shower was over.

On 5 August 1664, Pepys left London with a relation by marriage, W. Joyce, planning to meet his wife at Stevenage. Arrangements did not go according to plan:

> Thence forward to Barnett and there drank, and so by night to Stevenage, it raining a little but not much; and there to my great trouble find that my wife was not come, nor any Stamford coach gone down this week, so that she cannot come. So, vexed and weary . . . I after supper to bed. And after a little sleep, W. Joyce comes in his shirt to my chamber with a note and a messenger from my wife that she was come by York coach to Bigglesworth, and would be with me tomorrow morning. So, I mightily pleased at her discreet action in this busines, I with peace to sleep again till next morning . . . and W. Joyce and I to a game of Bowles on the green there – till 8 a'clock and then comes my wife in the coach, and a coach full of women. So, very joyful, drank there . . .

Later that same year on 15 October, Pepys, with W. Joyce, stayed once again at the Swan after a visit to his parents. Although 'mighty merry' he was very weary, because of so much horse riding, but he had made a useful discovery:

> I find that a coney skin in my breeches preserves me perfectly from galling – and that eating after I come to my inne, without drinking, doth keep me from being stomach-sick; which drink doth presently make me. We lay in several beds in the same room . . .

On 11 October 1667, Pepys had a nerve-racking journey from his father's house to Stevenage; he had some gold to transport and was in continual fear of robbers. He put the gold into a basket, which he placed under his seat in the coach, bending down to check it every 15 minutes:

> . . . and we straight to Stevenage, through Baldock lanes, which are already very bad. And at Stevenage we came well before night, and all safe; and there with great care I got the gold up to the chamber, my wife carrying one bag and the girl another and W. Hewer the rest in the basket and set it under a bed in our chamber . . . and so anon to supper, and very merry we were and a good supper; and after supper to bed. Brecocke [Bococke] alive still and the best host I know about.

On one of his journeys through Hertfordshire, Pepys noticed that straw hats were often worn there. This was the beginning of the rise of the straw plait industry which was to become so important to the working people of Hertfordshire and Bedfordshire during the next two centuries. By the end of the seventeenth century straw plait was already being sold at Hitchin market. Pepys' last reference to Stevenage is dated 5 June 1668, when he noted that he paid 5s. 6d. for dinner.

There were by now many inns along the High Street in Stevenage. Although the Swan at this time may have been the biggest, and certainly had an excellent reputation, it was rivalled in local importance by the White Lion. This inn was situated on the other side of the High Street, at the point where the road broadened out to leave a wide space where the cattle market was held, conveniently near a pond. In 1662 the landlord, William Welch, died and the White Lion was inherited by his daughter, Anne Welch. The Falcon, one of the High Street's oldest inns, was mentioned in the court sessions rolls of 1666, when Mathew Waterford of Stevenage was accused of 'stopping of a watercourse that formerly, for 40 years, ran out of the Falcon yard in Stevenage through Mathew Waterford's entry into the highway.'

The office of parish constable continued to be filled by annual election, but was not always carried out diligently. In 1667 Richard Wootton of Stevenage, labourer, was accused of 'denying to watch and ward at his turn there for the whole year last past.' Another townsman failing in his public duty was George Chapman of Stevenage who, in 1668, apparently did not repair 'a road there, in a place called "le Backlane" near a close called "Backlane".' Other Stevenage citizens ignored planning regulations, to their cost. In 1684 the magistrates issued a certificate that John Andrews of Stevenage who was lately indicted for erecting a cottage and not laying four acres of ground to it, has pulled down the said cottage.

While these parochial matters were occupying people locally, on a national level the monarchy was again in trouble. Eventually, in 1688, the pro-Catholic King James II was officially considered to have abdicated and the so-called Glorious Revolution brought his daughter, Mary, and her husband, the Protestant William of Orange, to the throne. Stevenage may or may not have approved, but no doubt there was general approbation in the town when the market was revived in 1694, by royal charter from William and Mary. As the seventeenth century drew to a close, Stevenage was poised for a period of growth and prosperity.

CHAPTER FIVE

The Eighteenth Century and the Coaching Era

By the turn of the century the recently revived Stevenage market had become almost exclusively a cattle market, for beasts driven on the hoof from Scotland and Wales towards London. The market was largely frequented by drovers and butchers. The open space in the High Street, between the White Lion and the Old Castle Inn at the top of Middle Row, provided a suitable stopping place for the cattle as there was room to accommodate them and a convenient pond in a field behind the White Lion. In fact, the High Street was well supplied with ponds, from the one near the Bowling Green to those at the south end where Holy Trinity church now stands. The ponds were connected by a ditch running the length of the High Street, no doubt welcomed by the weary cattle, but not ideal for humans, as it was used for refuse of all kinds.

The High Street in 1700 was lined by many wooden houses, and a considerable number of buildings which are still standing today. The old schoolhouse of Alleyne's Grammar School, the nearby maltings, the Swan Inn (now the Grange), the Bowling Green, much of Middle Row and several other inns were all in existence at this time. The most noticeable differences to a modern eye would be the rutted, unpaved, undrained road running in a straight line from the Bowling Green to London, the absence of trees which now line the street and the presence of farmyards and fields between or immediately behind the buildings.

The first historian of the county, Henry Chauncy, published his *History of Hertfordshire* in 1700. He had been a pupil at Alleyne's Grammar School during the Civil War and his family home was Ardley Bury, so he may have had a special interest in the Stevenage district. He gave some space to the deserted village of Box in his book, stating 'there was anciently a church belonging to the same in a field on the hill near the woods now called the churchyard and where the foundations may be seen'.

Another observer of the Hertfordshire scene was Daniel Defoe, best remembered for *Robinson Crusoe*, who noted in his *Tour through the Whole Island of Great Britain* in 1704 that Hertfordshire had several characters:

> That part of it adjoining to Bedfordshire and Buckinghamshire is Whiggish and full of Dissenters. That part adjoining to Huntingdonshire, Cambridgeshire and Essex entirely Church and all of the High sort.

Under this sweeping generalization Stevenage falls into the first section and it is certainly true that, following the Toleration Act of 1689 which made it legal for Dissenters (i.e. non-Anglicans) to practise their faith, a number of Stevenage people were recorded as belonging to other sects, including that of the Quakers. The influence of John Bunyan, who had often preached in the villages of north Hertfordshire, was also strong in Stevenage.

The Toleration Act required the registration of places used for non-Anglican religious worship and the following entry appeared in the Stevenage register for 1709:

> These are to certify that a barn standing in the yard belonging to the dwelling house of William Bradley in Stevenage and also one other barn in Stevenage, aforesaid, which the said Wm. Bradley holds of John Langthorne of Ashwell are respectively appointed for places of worship for Protestant Dissenters, commonly called Quakers, this 18th day of the 3rd month, called May, 1709. [Until 1752 March was the first month of the year.]

Avenue, leading from the
h Street, through Bury
ad, to St Nicholas' church,
9. The middle section of
Avenue was planted with
se-chestnuts and limes in
6 by Rector Nicholas
olwell.

Although Quakers and other non-conformists were now free to worship openly, the Church of England remained at the centre of parish life. It is possible that some rectors, over the centuries, may have been absent from the parish and paid other priests to undertake the bare minimum of religious duties, but there is no evidence of this. Stevenage was fortunate in having a number of outstanding rectors, who contributed much to the town. One of these was Nicholas Cholwell, who was incumbent from 1738 to 1773. He took a lively and benevolent interest in the town and kept a detailed 'Memorandum Book', which has proved invaluable to historians. It was during his time that the middle section of the path from the High Street, through Bury Mead to St Nicholas' church, was planted with limes and horse chestnuts to form a gracious avenue.

Greater religious tolerance, together with an increasing understanding of scientific principles, was helping people generally to move away from much of the superstition of previous centuries, such as belief in witchcraft and the cruel persecution that accompanied it. North Hertfordshire, however, appears to have been sadly backward in this respect. In 1711 England's last trial for witchcraft concerned a Walkern woman. Old Jane Wenham, who had the misfortune to live alone with a black cat for company, was committed to trial on suspicion of being a witch by none other than the historian Sir Henry Chauncy. The jury found her guilty, but reason prevailed in the person of Judge Powell, who ordered her release and ensured that she was then found a safe and peaceful home in which to end her days. A pamphlet written by the principal witness against her, the Revd Francis Bragge, Vicar of Hitchin, achieved wide circulation in the district, helping shamefully to fan the dying flames of persecution.

The country's economic problems and the expense of European wars forced eighteenth-century governments to look for new ways of raising money. One was the Window Tax, by which householders were taxed according to the number of windows in their houses. Some people reacted by bricking up some of their windows to reduce the amount of money they had to pay. Records show that in Stevenage in 1715 there were 116 houses liable to this tax, 3 of them with 30 or more windows, 5 with 20 or more, 36 with 10 or more and 72 with fewer than 10. The initial rate seems to have been 10s. for houses with 20 or more windows, 6s. for those with 10 or more and 2s. for those with under 10, but subsequently a 'new' tax was added to the higher bands, increasing the levy to £1 10s. for houses with over 30 windows and to £1 for those with over 20.

During this period, Hertfordshire was enjoying something of a property boom, as London businessmen paid high prices for houses in the county, which they then endeavoured to keep as a haven of rural peace, probably using their influence to discourage the introduction of industry. This is all the more surprising in view of the fact that the eighteenth century was the greatest period of road improvement since Roman times. For Stevenage and similar towns in Hertfordshire, however, the new roads did not bring industrial development, but simply made it easier to transport vast quantities of agricultural produce to London and to bring back refuse and manure to fertilize the soil.

mond Hill chalk pit
ow Providence Grove),
1700–99. Some men are
ning chalk, others loading
art.

It was in another part of Hertfordshire that the first turnpiked road had been established. In 1663 parliament passed an Act putting the repair and maintenance of a section of Ermine Street (the old North Road, later A10) under the control of the Justices of Hertfordshire, Cambridgeshire and Huntingdonshire, because the parishes through which it passed were unable to maintain it. This stretch of road was so heavily used by wagons loaded with barley on their way to the malting town of Ware, and at the same time so neglected, that it had become a public danger. To pay for the repairs, the Justices were empowered to install turnpikes, manned by toll-keepers, to ensure that travellers paid for the privilege of using the road. But it was not until the eighteenth century that 'turnpiking' of roads became widespread.

Each Turnpike Trust, set up by Act of Parliament, was made up of a group of businessmen who contributed some of their own capital and were permitted to raise additional sums from investors. They then employed surveyors and road builders to improve the stretch of road for which they were responsible and hoped to recover their outlay and make a profit from the tolls payable at the turnpikes. There was no provision for the care of the complete length of a road, which was a drawback, but at least the Turnpike Trusts converted roads which had often been no more than pot-holed dirt tracks, dusty in summer and deep in mud in winter, into properly surfaced highways. As a result, travelling time from London to major cities was reduced dramatically, sometimes by as much as a third.

The road from London through Stevenage to the north (not yet known as the Great North Road) was turnpiked in sections. In 1712 a trust was established for the Highgate to Barnet stretch and this was extended in 1720 to just south of Potters Bar. In June 1720 the Stevenage and Biggleswade Turnpike Trust was set up to administer the 13 miles of road from Stevenage through Baldock to Biggleswade and in 1726 yet another trust took responsibility for the section from Lemsford Mill via Hatfield to Stevenage. The Hertford to Broadwater Trust was not established until 1757.

The trustees of the Stevenage and Biggleswade Trust held their business meetings at one of the inns along their stretch of road. On 18 July 1730 five trustees were present: Pulter Forester, Edward Sparhauke, Angell Chauncy, the Revd Thomas Stamper, Rector of Stevenage, and Robert Gelsthorp. On this occasion they had to deal with a complaint concerning:

> . . . damages done in the ground of Mr Pratt by digging and carrying away the gravel from the pit and the surveyors, Mr Glenister and Mr Manason, have computed the said damages at five pounds. Ordered that the treasurer of this turnpike do pay the said Pratt £50 [sic] in full of their share of the said damages.

Very few of the turnpike trusts were profitable. The Stevenage and Biggleswade Trust, meeting on 29 September 1730 at the Royal Oak in Biggleswade, drew up a petition to parliament requesting limitations on the weight of wagons and additional tolls. They explained:

> that from the time the said Act was put in execution the said roads have been kept in good repair until winter last when they were so much impaired that they became almost as ruinous as if they had never been amended, occasioned chiefly by ye prodigious and excessive weights and burthens, quantities of wheat flour, barley and malt most commonly sixty or seventy

hundredweight in a waggon and many of them go so loaded thro' ye said road twice in a day paying only the single duty.

That the materials for mending the said roads are very indifferent (the gravel being small) and loamy and stones being scarce and by no means the consistance sufficient to resist the pressure of such immoderate weights. . . .

Despite their cogent argument, the trustees' request was refused. They had other problems, some of their own making, such as the difficulty of achieving a quorate meeting. The minute book often recorded 'There being not a sufficient number of trustees present no business was transacted.' Ensuring adequate supplies of gravel was a continual worry and there are many records of negotiations between the trustees and local farmers and landowners for permission to extract gravel on their land. On 30 August 1745 the trustees, meeting at the White Horse, Baldock, resolved 'that the treasurer do pay to Mr Benjamin Lawrence two pounds, six shillings and sixpence for twenty poles of land near Stevenage Turnpike where a gravel pit has lately been opened. . . .'

As part of their road improvement programme, each turnpike trust placed milestones along its route, for the benefit of travellers. Three of the Stevenage and Biggleswade Trust's milestones can still be seen on the Great North Road out of Stevenage, one just south of Rectory Lane, another to the south of Graveley and the third on the south side of Jack's Hill.

The Stevenage turnpike, or toll-gate, was just north of the town, between Rectory Lane and Corey's Mill Lane. There was a toll-house there, occupied by a series of gatekeepers, including John Draper and Thomas Crawley, but even so it was reported in 1733 that certain crafty waggoners 'do frequently avoid paying at Stevenage turnpike by going out of this road. . . .' The trustees therefore resolved to set up an additional turnpike in Graveley parish, to catch the dodgers.

Near the Stevenage turnpike was a small alehouse, no doubt popular with travellers, which, since the beginning of the eighteenth century, had been known as the Marquess of Granby. In 1756 Robert Thurgood, a brewer of Baldock, took out a mortgage on the property and paid it off within a few years.

The Stevenage and Biggleswade Trust had another turnpike at the New Inn and the trustees seem to have transferred toll-keepers from one to another, whether or not as promotion is not clear. Toll-keepers at the New Inn included John Rudd, John Draper, who was later transferred to Stevenage turnpike, and Ebenezer Moss. The

Stevenage turnpike house needed repair in 1745 and the trustees 'ordered that the ground floor of Stevenage turnpike house be forthwith repaired and amended in such a manner as Mr Smith, Mr Needham and Mr Cholwell [Rector of Stevenage] shall think fit.'

It became common practice for trusts to engage the services of a professional 'toll-farmer', who paid an agreed fixed annual sum of money to a trust and then made his income from the tolls his men collected at the turnpike. Some farmers took advantage of the obvious opportunities for swindling either the travelling public, or the trustees, or both. The Watton Turnpike Trust, established in 1757 to improve the road from Hertford to Broadwater, was one of those that engaged a toll-farmer. This trust was small and so unprofitable that eventually the farmer went bankrupt. The trust was unable to find anyone else willing to take on the task and so the trustees were forced to make their own arrangements for collecting the tolls.

As the roads improved, so did transport vehicles. Stage-coaches, which were improved versions of covered wagons, often quite luxurious in design, were drawn by teams of specially bred horses and ran to strict timetables along the major roads. There was great competition between stage-coach companies and when a coach stopped at an inn the driver expected a fresh team of horses to be ready for immediate harnessing into the shafts for the next stage of the journey. The first regular stage-coach recorded as serving Stevenage was *The Perseverance* in 1741. The service was started by John Shrimpton, whose family were to continue it for over one hundred years. An early advertisement announced:

Hitchin and Bedford
Stage coaching in one day! Sets out from the Greyhound Inn in Smithfield, London, every Tuesday, Thursday and Saturday to the Sun Inn at Hitchin and returns for London every Monday, Wednesday and Friday. Also goes every Tuesday morning AT THREE OF THE CLOCK precisely from the Greyhound Inn aforesaid to the Swan Inn, Bedford and returns every Wednesday from [sic] London and goes through Hatfield, Welling, Stevenage, Hitchin, Alicey, Hendlow, Southill, Old Warden and Coalington to Bedford.
　　　Performed (if God permit)
　　　by John Shrimpton.

Dick Turpin, scourge of the Great North Road, is reputed to have escaped justice more than once by hiding in a secret passage in the

Swan Inn. The passage was still in existence in the 1940s to the delight of children from the Briar Patch Children's Home who were living there at the time, but it was blocked up to prevent them coming to harm. The other highwayman with Stevenage connections was James Whitney, who is said to have taken his name from Whitney Wood. However, historians point out that neither Dick Turpin nor Whitney were as glamorous as they have been painted. The famous ride from London to York was not carried out by Turpin but by William Nevison, and Whitney, far from being a 'gentleman', was a butcher and grazier.

Among the many coaching inns that lined the High Street in addition to the famous Swan, was the Yorkshire Grey. In 1754 it was occupied by James Mason and Wright Titmus and in 1786 it was bought by the prosperous Baldock brewer, John Pryor. As well as barns and stables, the property included about 18 acres of land. The White Lion had even more land, about 30 acres in 1774, when it also had many barns and outhouses and stabling for thirty horses. Even so, it had one drawback as a coaching inn; its main gateway was too low for coaches to pass through into the yard and so they had to be loaded and unloaded in the adjacent open space. The White Lion's assembly room was a favourite meeting-place for the Stevenage Vestry (forerunner of the local council) and for other official bodies.

About 100 yards further down, the Falcon and the Red Lion were still flourishing, although it seems that during the eighteenth century the Falcon's trade dwindled and it was taken over by its more successful neighbour. Almost opposite, on the other side of the High Street, was the Fox, occupied by John Tamplin in the second half of the century until 1784 when it was added to John Pryor's empire. Not far away was the White Hart, probably a wooden building, and at the south end, facing a pond, was the New Inn, occupied in 1786 by William Mayes. On the other side of the road stood the Chequers, a property owned by the Lyttons of Knebworth and leased in 1774 to Thomas Whittington. At that time it was far more than an inn, having a farm of 40 acres and a slaughterhouse attached.

As well as the big coaching inns and smaller hostelries there were many other houses where ale was brewed and refreshment purveyed under licence, or sometimes without. One such establishment was a cottage, with brewhouse, owned in 1793 by Joseph Emery and later known as the Marquess of Lorne. It was situated opposite the open space in front of Southend Farm, where the town's straw plait market was held.

Many Stevenage people made their livings from occupations associated with innkeeping. Coopers, who made beer barrels, were much in demand. Various members of the Moulden family, who lived in Stevenage during the second half of the eighteenth century, were occupied in several related trades. James and Simon Moulden were coopers, two other Moulden brothers were brewers and another two were butchers. Another trade often mentioned in eighteenth-century Stevenage records was that of the blacksmith. Apart from the many people who earned their living as servants, most of the rest of the population were employed in some kind of farm work. Considering its size, its importance as a coaching stop on the Great North Road and its proximity to London, the predominantly rural and agricultural nature of Stevenage is perhaps a little surprising. A number of the houses in the High Street were in fact farmhouses, with cattleyards immediately behind them, opening into fields beyond.

There were inns and alehouses in most of the roads leading from the High Street. In Walkern Road stood the Royal Oak where Stevenage Vestry meetings were held for a time. It was built of wood and had a paddock. The licensee in 1752 was William Bennett. Further along the Walkern Road, about a mile out of the town, stood the Three Horseshoes at Pin Green. William Spencer, the licensee in 1773, had a notice of complaint served against him for 'harbouring people on Sundays'. What became of him subsequently is not known, but in 1792 the Three Horseshoes became yet another of John Pryor's acquisitions. Pryor also bought an adjoining cottage and enlarged the inn. At Broadwater, where the Great North Road of the Welwyn Turnpike Trust was joined by the Watton Trust's road from Hertford, stood the Roebuck Inn, well known to travellers including Dick Turpin, so legend has it.

On the road from Stevenage to Hitchin, at the corner of the lane linking the Hitchin Road with the Great North Road, which had been used by devious coachmen to avoid paying tolls at the Stevenage turnpike, stood a small cluster of dwellings around Corey's Mill. The Henry Corey after whom the mill and the lane were named, had been miller here a century earlier. He had married a widow, Anne Tattershall. In 1613 she was taken to court, accused of poisoning her former husband, John Tattershall. Evidence against her was given by Dr Thomas Gornye of Hitchin, Leonard Tattershall of London, tallow chandler, and Robert Tattershall of Ardeley, clerk. Whatever the outcome, the case must have been a talking point in Stevenage for many years.

A beerhouse known as the Harrow existed at Corey's Mill in the eighteenth century, if not earlier. By 1769 its name had been

Corey's Mill. (Watercolour by Samuel Lucas, *c*. 1900.)

changed to the White Horse, and it belonged to a blacksmith, Nathan Cooke, who took out a mortgage on it in that year. In the following centuries its name was changed several times.

Windmills were another familiar sight in the district. For centuries there had been a mill on the high ground near St Nicholas' church, in a field still known until recently as Mill Field, off Almonds Lane. It was on this high ground, near Mill Field, that a row of Pest Houses was built in 1765, to provide an isolation hospital for smallpox victims. This highly infectious disease was rife in the eighteenth century, but Hertfordshire was unusually fortunate in that its MP from 1767 was the Quaker, Baron Thomas Dimsdale, a scientist and doctor who pioneered the technique of inoculation against smallpox. He published a treatise on the subject and travelled to Russia to inoculate the Empress Catherine the Great and her son, the Grand Duke Paul, following which he was awarded the Russian title of Baron. On his return to England he set up an inoculation clinic in Hertford.

In spite of general prosperity, eighteenth-century Stevenage had its problems and its share of poverty. Periodically throughout the century the country as a whole suffered from epidemics of smallpox and fever, shortages of food, low wages and high prices and other social ills which inevitably affected the poor most severely, and particularly the old. Following the Act of Parliament of 1722, which

45

Henry Trigg's coffin in the rafters of his barn behind the Old Castle Inn (now National Westminster Bank), 1955.

permitted parishes to set up workhouses, or poorhouses, to shelter and occupy their homeless poor, Stevenage decided to establish its own workhouse. On 9 May 1722 the Stevenage Vestry meeting recorded an agreement with Henry Trigg, of the Old Castle Inn, to pay him £1 10s. rent annually for the use of his barn, which backed on to Back Lane, as a parish workhouse.

Before alterations and improvements to the barn could be completed Henry Trigg died, leaving instructions in his will that his body should not be buried, but placed in its coffin on the rafters of his barn. It is probable that he wished to avoid the attentions of the grave-robbers, who lurked in churchyards after dark to remove newly buried bodies and sell them to medical students for anatomical research. Trigg's coffin remains in the rafters, as he willed, and has become a tourist attraction.

The Stevenage Vestry was now unable to take over the barn as it had planned, but fortunately George Crouch, churchwarden and member of the vestry, came to the rescue with the offer of a building of his own and by December 1724 the Stevenage Workhouse was in being. The inmates were provided with equipment and materials to enable them to earn money by spinning and weaving. In 1726 the Overseers of the Poor were ordered to buy a second-hand copper plus tubs and utensils to brew small beer for the poor in the workhouse, an indication, perhaps, that the Stevenage Vestry did not believe in too harsh a regime.

It was not long before the number of paupers reached twelve and George Crouch's house was too small to accommodate any more. The vestry looked for a larger property and tried to reach agreement with Alice Green to buy her house on Letchmore Green. They were unsuccessful and it was not until 1773 that a solution was found. In that year the vestry bought a house situated not far from Letchmore Green, facing the pond at the south end of the High Street, and which had formerly been the home of John Hitchin, a butcher. This building continued as the parish workhouse for nearly a century, later also acquiring the parish lock-up in its grounds.

In addition to poverty and disease, eighteenth-century Stevenage residents had one other great fear. If a fire was to break out, which was liable to happen at any time, it would consume the wooden houses which made up most of the town. Stevenage seems to have been particularly unfortunate with regard to this. In 1763 the parish acquired a fire-engine with a treadle pump, worked by three men using feet and hands. It cannot have been very efficient or very manoeuvrable and it certainly did not save the alehouse (later known as the Two Diamonds) next to the Yorkshire Grey, which burnt down at the end of the century.

In 1795 a survey presented to the Board of Agriculture deemed Hertfordshire 'the first corn county in England'. Reference was made to the widespread local practice of chalking the soil – that is, digging pits from which chalk was hauled in baskets and then dragged across the fields and spread on the clay and flint to make it more fertile. There were many such pits in the Stevenage districts, some of which are still visible today.

While the men were labouring in the fields, a small revolution was taking place in their homes as women found that such was the demand for straw plait that they could earn as much, if not more than their husbands. Children, too, could make money from this skill and many attended straw plait schools, to the detriment of a more academic education. There was a feeling among the middle and upper classes that the financial independence bestowed by the sale of straw plait was not a good thing. It made the poor 'saucy' and less inclined to take work as servants. On the other hand, it did mean that they were more able to look after themselves and this kept the poor rate low.

irlands Farm, 1804.
ainting by H.G. Oldfield.)

CHAPTER SIX

The Victorian Age

In 1801 the first British national population census recorded that there were 1,254 people living in Stevenage, of whom 330 were in employment – 229 working in agriculture and the remaining 101 in trades or crafts. There were 258 occupied dwelling houses within the 4,545 acres that were contained within the parish boundaries. Hitchin, the chief town of north Hertfordshire, had a population of 3,161 and an acreage of 6,420. Graveley's population was 260 and its acreage 1,838, while Shephall had 120 people and an acreage of 1,156.

During the early years of the nineteenth century Stevenage suffered more than ever from destruction by fire. In 1804 the White Lion was partially burnt, but apparently escaped unscathed during the Great Fire of Stevenage, which broke out on Friday 10 July 1807 in a wheelwright's shop at the corner of Walkern Road and the High Street, destroying many of the nearby wooden buildings. The fire flared up again two days later and this time property around the Swan Inn was badly damaged, including a maltings, stores of malt and many straw and hay ricks. Cass, landlord of the Swan, lost outhouses, nine haystacks and two straw ricks to the fire. As so often happens with disasters, crowds of sightseers came to Stevenage. One of them, John Carrington, a Bramfield farmer, recorded in his diary, 'Saw upwards of 40 houses with their offices all down . . . a vast many people there to see the ruins.'

The little Stevenage fire-engine with its treadle pump was completely inadequate to deal with this conflagration and help was summoned from Hitchin, where there were four companies of Volunteers. Captain Thomas Wilshere and Lieutenant John Bedford led the company which came to Stevenage and their task was probably as much to stop any possible looting as to fight the fire. While in Stevenage they were called to the White Lion by the landlord who had found an intruder in one of the bedrooms. He was forcibly removed by Captain Wilshere and Lieutenant Bedford and taken, with the aid of a constable, to the lock-up at the south end of the town. Unfortunately, in spite of his questionable behaviour, he later sued the officers and won damages of £40. This, added to the £5 11s. payable to the duty

Stevenage Fire Brigade with its horse-drawn fire cart in Church Lane, 1890.

firemen, made it an expensive night for the Hitchin Volunteers, although they did receive £50 from Stevenage.

At midnight on 3 October 1829 another major fire occurred, starting in the yard of the White Hart at the south end of the High Street. The inn itself, all the horses in the stables and ten neighbouring houses were destroyed. After this second tragedy the Stevenage Vestry decided to purchase a new and· improved fire-engine, which they did in 1831, together with an engine house in Back Lane.

These two great fires changed the appearance of the High Street, as reconstruction work was carried out using bricks and mortar to replace the former wooden or lath and plaster buildings. Much of the building material was supplied locally, from the brickworks in and around Stevenage, such as the one not far from the south end and now immortalized in the name Brick Kiln Road. There was another at Six Hills, owned by John Matthews.

Undeterred by the ravages of fire and subsequent reconstruction, the coaches which hurtled up and down the Great North Road continued to use Stevenage as an important staging post. Some of the town's inns, such as the White Lion, the Red Lion and the Old Castle, had escaped the fire altogether. Others were rebuilt and quickly resumed their business. There were some changes of name and ownership; by 1806 the New Inn, at the south end, was kept by Thomas Favill and renamed the Coach and Horses. In 1813 it was bought by John Crabb, a Hitchin brewer, and by 1841 it had stabling for twenty-five horses. The Chequers, on the opposite side of the road, was leased in 1820 to the St Albans brewers, Searancke and Steward, although it was still owned by the Lyttons.

The ubiquitous John Pryor continued steadily to buy up local inns. In 1821 he purchased the Red Lion. The old Falcon next door had been closed as a separate establishment in about 1800. Pryor already owned) the Fox opposite and by 1806 had changed its name to the Unicorn.

Of all the High Street inns in the nineteenth century, the White Lion had perhaps the most historic role. During the Napoleonic Wars, between 1793 and 1815, French prisoners were marched through the High Street on their way to jail, many ending up at the large prisoner-of-war camp at Norman Cross in Huntingdonshire. The White Lion's barns and outhouses, heavily guarded, often provided shelter and the opportunity of a night's rest for the weary Frenchmen.

Along the main roads turnpike trusts continued trying to recoup their expenses from tolls. For charging purposes road users were divided into numerous categories including: hogs, sheep, or lambs; horses, mules and asses; oxen or meat cattle; wagons and carts, charged per horse; two-, three- or six-horse coaches and chaises. The Stevenage Turnpike toll-book for 1811 recorded that the average takings per week were between £26 and £33.

Coaches which passed through Stevenage during the first thirty years of the nineteenth century included *The Express* (W. Chaplin and Co.), which took twenty-one-and-a-half hours to cover the 167 miles from the Spreadeagle, Gracechurch Street, London, to Barton-upon-Humber via Waltham Cross, Hertford, Stevenage, Baldock, Norman Cross, Peterborough and Lincoln. *The Perseverance* continued to run from the King's Arms, Snow Hill, London, via Barnet, Hatfield, Stevenage, Biggleswade, Huntingdon, Peterborough and Spalding. *The Union* ran from either Regent Circus or Golden Cross through Barnet, Stevenage, Baldock, Stamford, Grantham, Doncaster and Wakefield to Leeds, covering a distance of 191 miles in twenty-four hours. Its rival, *The Rockingham*, started from the Saracen's Head, Snow Hill, followed an apparently identical route calculated to be 190 miles long, and claimed a journey time of twenty-three hours.

Even during this time, the heyday of the coaching era, when the turnpiked roads were constantly crowded with traffic, the turnpike trusts were finding it difficult to balance their books, let alone make the substantial profits they had anticipated. Upkeep of the roads was a continuous drain on their resources. Trusts were empowered to employ labourers themselves but many, including the Stevenage Trust, still relied on statute labour for some or all of their maintenance work. On 29 October 1813, Isaac Hindley, gentleman and treasurer to the Stevenage Trust, applied to two local Justices of the Peace, Adolphus Meetherke and Henry Baker, Rector of Stevenage, to serve notice of statute duty to be carried out

> on such days and times (not being hay-time or harvest) and on such parts of the said road within the said parish of Stevenage as the said trustees or their surveyor shall from time to time order, direct and appoint.

Those summoned on this occasion and the labour they were required to provide were: Mary Cass (30 days), John Smith (15 days), Edward Parkins (10 days), George Newman (8 days), Thomas Stalley (7 days), William Stratton (5 days), each to supply one team and one able man. Statute labour was not only understandably unpopular, but also inadequate to the needs of road users and at last, in 1835, it was abolished.

It was the railway which eventually brought about the end of the coaching era and with it the collapse of the turnpike trusts as takings at toll-gates plummeted. When plans for a railway from London to York were under discussion there was a proposal, which received considerable support, to route the line from Welwyn via Kimpton to the centre of Hitchin. Local landowners opposed this and instead the Great Northern Railway took the course which it follows today, through Knebworth and Stevenage. This line, from King's Cross to Peterborough, was opened in 1850 and later in the same year Stevenage station was opened. Queen Victoria graced the railway company with her presence by making a royal train journey along the new line. Hitchin station was extravagantly decorated with straw plait for the occasion.

Stevenage station was sited near Julian's Farm, between the Hitchin road and Fisher's Green. A new road was built, leading from the High Street to the station, with the name Railway Street. It soon earned itself a reputation as a place of ill-repute and was subsequently improved and renamed Orchard Road.

The railway gave Stevenage quick and easy communication with London and, through the extensive network of branch lines that sprang up, with many other places, such as Bedford, which are now no longer accessible by rail from Stevenage. Although road transport and the coaching trade declined, more people came into the town, some to settle in the new houses which were being built along the London and Hitchin roads. On the other hand, the ancient markets lost their importance as even cattle were transported by rail and the fair, which in 1821 had been transferred to 22 September, changed steadily into a fair purely for pleasure. Stevenage High Street, like that of many another country town, fell into a state of decline as coaching inns were no longer in demand, leaving those employed in related trades with little or no work.

The novelist Charles Dickens, a friend of Sir Edward Bulwer Lytton, often came by train to visit him at Knebworth. Dickens knew Stevenage quite well. His story *Tom Tiddler's Ground*, published in 1861, begins with a description of Stevenage High Street, telling how desolate it appeared in those post-coaching days. Looking out from an inn he called 'The Peal of Bells', which he probably based on the White Hart in Stevenage High Street, he commented:

The White Hart, *c.* 1958. This was probably the inn referred to as the Peal of Bells in Dickens' story *Tom Tiddler's Ground.*

> The village street was like most other village streets: wide for its height, silent for its size and drowsy in the dullest degree . . . a score of weak little lath-and-plaster cabins clung in confusion about the Attorney's red-brick house . . . some of the small tradesmen's houses, such as the crockery shop and the harness-maker's, had a cyclops window in the middle of the gable. . . .

The 'Tom Tiddler's Ground' of the story was the piece of land at Redcoats Green, along the road from Stevenage through Fisher's Green and Todds Green, where the famous hermit James Lucas lived for years locked inside his house. He peered out from a barred window to converse with the many sightseers who came to stare at him, as if on an outing to the zoo. Lucas was the son of a wealthy Hitchin family, whose eccentricity was made worse by the death of his mother, after which he withdrew from normal society into self-imposed imprisonment. He is reputed by some local people to have had healing powers and by others to possess great wisdom; certainly he was an educated man. However, he ignored the great Charles Dickens, refusing to converse with him and sending him unceremoniously on his way.

Dickens had his revenge in *Tom Tiddler's Ground* by depicting Lucas as Mr Mopes, a filthy and foolish man who, like a metal that rusts away from want of care or use, was best left to rot. The modern public house, the Tom Tiddler, in Symonds Green, commemorates the story, albeit rather confusingly. It is sited some 2 miles from the authentic location and implies that Tom Tiddler was a person, whereas Dickens was referring to a children's game.

In 1845 Dickens formed an amateur theatrical company to raise money for charity and when, in 1850, his friend, Bulwer Lytton, proposed a Dramatic Festival at Knebworth, he agreed enthusiastically to take part. For three evenings in November 1850 the rich and great of the county flocked to Knebworth to see a performance of Ben Jonson's *Every Man in his Humour*, followed by a farce. Both public-spirited men, Dickens and Bulwer Lytton decided to give practical help to impecunious writers and artists by building a group of dwellings where they could live as a community. The rural peace and quiet and freedom from financial pressures would, so the philanthropists believed, enable the free flow of creative inspiration. Bulwer Lytton gave a piece of land on the Great North Road just past the Six Hills, on the way into Stevenage and for the next fifteen years Dickens and Bulwer Lytton worked determinedly to raise money for their scheme, which they called the Guild of Arts and Literature.

The plan was to pay a warden £200 per year, plus housing, and to grant residents £170 per year and non-residents £200. There was also to be provision for promising young men (women do not appear to have been considered) to be granted £100 per year as 'Associates'. Bulwer Lytton wrote a play entitled *Not so Bad as We Seem*, which was taken on tour by Dickens with great success, raising £4,000 between 1851 and 1852. Dickens also donated the royalties from his novel *Bleak House*, which he dedicated to the Guild. By 1861 it was possible to begin building the Guild houses and Bulwer Lytton, in his capacity as an MP, succeeded in steering a charter of incorporation through parliament.

On Saturday 29 July 1865, the formal dedication of the Guild houses took place. Dickens and a party of his family and friends, including the writer Wilkie Collins, travelled by train to Stevenage station and thence by road to Knebworth House for lunch in the banqueting hall, where about 150 people were present. Speeches were made and reported in full in *The Times*. Dickens took the opportunity of praising his host, friend and fellow-novelist, Bulwer Lytton, saying of him, 'When the wealth, life and beauty now overflowing these halls shall have fled, crowds of people will come to see the place where he lived and wrote. . . .'

When the ceremonial opening of the Guild houses had taken place, it is reported that some of the literary guests took the opportunity of sampling the hospitality of the newly built public house on the opposite side of the Great North Road. Called the Mutual Friend it celebrated the friendship of Dickens and Bulwer Lytton.

After all the generosity and hard work the Guild of Arts and Literature was a failure. Artists and writers did not wish, as one put it, 'to be buried alive in Stevenage'. In 1897 the Guild houses were sold and the proceeds, together with remaining funds of £2,000, were divided between the Royal Literary Fund and the Artists' General Benevolent Institution.

Bulwer Lytton was a liberal and a supporter of social reform. He was one of those who advocated changing the rules of entry to the civil service and he supported the bill to widen voting rights which became the 1832 Reform Act. In 1852, as Lord Lytton, he was elected as one of the MPs for the County of Hertford.

The mid- and late nineteenth-century was a time of great and much-needed social reform, from practicalities to do with public health and hygiene to the law, education and ethical matters. Education for all children, not just those whose parents could afford to pay, became an increasingly important objective to many in Victorian society. Stevenage had its Grammar School, founded by Thomas Alleyne, but apart from that most children from working families had only the straw plait schools, where there was little in the way of 'book-learning' although probably the children did not mind too much.

It was recorded in 1817 that girls in the Hitchin district were kept away from school and knew nothing but how to plait. There were at least two plait schools in Stevenage in the mid-nineteenth century; one at the south end, near the open plait market, and the other beside the Royal Oak in Walkern Road.

In 1834 a new school was built, under the auspices of the National Society, one of the two religious organizations which helped towns and villages throughout the country to provide for the education of all their children, however poor. The school building cost £709 3s. 11d. in total and most of this money was raised by local subscription. The new school was sited near Alleyne's Grammar School on the Bury Mead, the traditional site for education in Stevenage. Although it was not compulsory at this time to send children to school the rector, the Revd R.G. Baker, was very pleased with the response of local parents. Despite the weekly fee the newly opened school received 116 boys and 91 girls.

In subsequent years several improvements were made to the school and after the 1870 Education Act, which made it compulsory

The Mutual Friend public house, London Road, opposite the Guild of Literature and Art, c. 1940. The building shown here has since been demolished, but its name lives on in the public house in Broadwater.

for local authorities to provide education, a decision was made to increase the accommodation of the Stevenage National School, at a cost of £635, which sum would be raised by public subscription. The enlarged building would consist of

> two separate schools, one for boys under a certified master and another for girls under a certified mistress. The infants' school, being already under a certified mistress, will be continued as it is but with a change of room. Our three schools will thus be entitled to claim the Government Grant every year.

The state now increasingly took control of the funding and direction of education through a system of grants which depended on such matters as attendance and examination success, the infamous 'payment by results'. The Stevenage school authorities were considerably exercised by the difficulties of enforcing attendance and awaited each annual report by a government inspector with some trepidation.

In June 1872 the *Stevenage Parish Magazine* reported on a recent visit to the town's brickyards and plaiting schools, where many children were employed. The writer explained that there were new laws regulating the hours and conditions under which children could be employed 'for the purposes of trade or profit in any shape', and pointed out that the straw plait schools came into this category since the plait made there was sold for profit. The new law stated:

1. No child shall be employed under eight years of age.
2. No child under thirteen shall be employed for more than six and a half hours in a day.
3. Every child so employed shall be obliged to attend a day school for at least ten hours in every week.
4. A certificate of attendance at School must be obtained by the occupiee from the Schoolmaster every week.

It was noted that, following the inspector's visit, there had been some increase in attendance at the Stevenage National Schools.

Poor attendance continued to hinder the smooth running of the schools for many years. In July 1882 the report of Her Majesty's Inspector was

> very creditable to the Master and Mistresses . . . the very serious irregularity, however, in the attendance of the children

is made the matter of special remark. . . . It seems as though it would become necessary to employ a special officer to follow up truant boys and girls and to expose and put a stop to the carelessness of some parents in allowing their children to remain at home for other than truly *unavoidable* causes . . . but for this great hindrance to their good working, the Stevenage Schools would be known as the best Schools in the whole district.

A year later, in May 1883, the situation was little different. The inspector stated that the Stevenage schools compared favourably with any school in his district, but ' . . . he did complain seriously . . . of the special failing of our schools, namely the irregularity of the children's attendance.' The rector, the Revd William Jowitt, commented sadly that 73 girls and 40 boys were unable to be examined by the inspector because of the irregularity of their attendance, which resulted in a total loss to the schools of approximately £78 of government grant, at 14s. per head. He added, 'As payment to the Schools will now, after this month, depend almost entirely on the attendance, this loss would next year, under similar circumstances, be much heavier.'

For village children above the age of compulsory schooling there were some limited opportunities for them to continue their education locally, thanks to the charitable activities of the gentry. Girls' sewing classes were provided by ladies of the parish, 'intended for girls who have left the National School, who wish to keep up their needlework and writing until they go to service and to help those whose education has been neglected.'

In addition to the lessons there were occasional social events. At the Annual Tea, held in the school on 23 March 1882, Mrs Jowitt, the rector's wife, and Mrs Dunn, the doctor's wife, 'presided at the tea table' while other ladies waited upon the girls. Then there were games, a talk and 'some capital stories' by the rector and a magic lantern entertainment, including slides of Jumbo, John Gilpin and Diogenes, 'which were most amusing and caused much merriment.' Prizes were awarded for attendance, good needlework and writing and a special prize for Lizzie Leggatt 'who left the Class five years ago for service and has ever since remained in the same family.' Small amounts of money were paid to the girls for their needlework, the highest sum of 4s. 4d. being earned by Emily Leggatt.

Arrangements were also made for those in employment to go to evening classes, as advertised in November 1871:

Night School – All above 14 years of age who wish to attend the Night School during the approaching winter are requested to be at the National School on Monday the 6th at 7.30 o'clock.

For a few young people there was the possibility of taking up teaching as a career. An advertisement of July 1872 read:

Pupil Teachers – There is a favourable opening now for young persons to become pupil teachers, apprenticed under the sanction of the Government, in the Boys' and Girls' Schools. The master and mistress, both holding certificates from the Education Department are qualified to receive pupil teachers. They must be not less than 13 years of age.

The printed word was another means to education and small collections of books, often of a religious nature, were available through the various Sunday schools which existed in the town. For adults there was a parish library of 'something like three hundred volumes . . . ready to be in circulation during the autumn and winter months.' This facility existed for many years and was periodically enlarged by donation and organized by a succession of honorary librarians. Towards the end of the nineteenth century it was housed at the Rookery in the High Street, under the management of Miss Eadon. Membership at that time was by subscription of 1s. 6d. per year or 2d. per month and books could be exchanged every Tuesday from 12.15 to 12.45 p.m.

In 1847 the famous old coaching inn, the Swan, was put up for sale. The coaching trade having declined, this substantial building now had no future as an inn and, somewhat to the surprise of local people, it was bought by the Revd John Osborne Seager, to be converted into a boys' preparatory school. This caused some consternation among staff at Alleyne's Grammar School, not merely because the rival establishment was almost next door, but because the Revd Seager was head teacher at Alleyne's. However, the venture went ahead and the Swan Inn, renamed the Grange, was swiftly converted for use by schoolboys. It soon established itself as a preparatory school, enrolling such prestigious pupils as the future Earl of Chichester.

Throughout the nineteenth century the population of Stevenage increased steadily. A major development took place with the building of Albert Street, a completely new road linking Letchmore Road to the High Street. Albert Street, named after the Prince

Consort, was intended as a shopping street for the growing number of artisans in the town, and it also provided new houses for some of the people crowded into ancient cottages at Letchmore Green and Church Lane and for newcomers to the town. Other new roads were built, including Hellards and Alleyn's Roads, named after former rectors.

Not surprisingly, the people living in the new roads, even the most devout, objected to the long walk to St Nicholas' church and in 1861 a chapel-of-ease was built for the convenience of parishioners living some distance from the parish church. The new church was named Holy Trinity, after the old medieval guild of that name. By coincidence the lord of the manor of Stevenage, the Bishop of London of the day, was the brother of Canon Blomfield, Rector of Stevenage from 1834 to 1874. The bishop generously gave a plot of land at the south end of the town for the site of the church. Unfortunately the plot consisted largely of the pond in front of the Coach and Horses Inn and the workhouse. Farmers from nearby Southend Farm, Pound Farm and other local farms came to the rescue and arranged for cartloads of rubble to be tipped into the pond before building work started. One of those who helped was Joseph Piggott of Springfield Cottage just across the High Street behind the Chequers Inn. The architect was the rector's nephew, A.W. Blomfield.

Holy Trinity church, newly built in 1861.

At this time, in spite of the advance of science and sceptical anti-religious attitudes on the part of many intellecutals, the churches, particularly the Church of England, were very much at the forefront of society. Stevenage was typical in having, besides its rector and curate, a number of other ordained clergy who were employed as school teachers, private tutors, or in some other profession and who helped out at the numerous Sunday services and weekday religious gatherings. Each of the surrounding villages, Graveley, Little and Great Wymondley, Aston, Benington, Walkern and Weston, also had several Church of England clergy and they visited each other's churches as guest preachers at festivals, to give lectures, lead lent courses or to help organize social events. To a large extent the Church of England clergy and their wives were the equivalent of today's local councils and social services; they cared for the poor, the sick and the elderly and took a lead in the provision of education and leisure facilities as well as attending to the spiritual needs of the parish.

Although the Church of England may have appeared to dominate religious and social life, the nineteenth century saw a great increase in churches of other denominations. In Stevenage the Methodist Church grew steadily, inspired by the visit in 1790 of John Wesley, who preached in the High Street in his old age. After using rented

A view of the back of Stevenage Rectory in 1804, before the two wings were added later in the century. (Painting by H.G. Oldfield.)

former rectory, now
wn as the Priory, after the
tion of two wings,
876–86. (Photographed
Lawson Thompson.)

accommodation, including No. 38 High Street, the Stevenage Methodists were at last able to build their own church at the corner of Sish Lane and London Road, where previously they had held open-air services. The building was opened in 1876.

In 1829 the Catholic Emancipation Act had been passed and subsequently many new Roman Catholic churches were built throughout the country. In Stevenage, in due course, the Church of the Transfiguration was built in Grove Road, with a Roman Catholic rectory backing on to it in Basil's Road.

Baptists in Stevenage were sufficiently numerous to need two chapels, a substantial building with a schoolroom beside it in Basil's Road and a small Ebenezer chapel opened in Albert Street in 1857. One of the Albert Street Baptist preachers was Henry Fox, who lived in a cottage at Symond's Green. He and his wife were by all accounts devout and worthy people and when their twin sons were born in 1857, they named them Albert Ebenezer and Ebenezer Albert, after the little chapel where they worshipped.

No one has yet unravelled the mystery of why the Fox twins grew up to be poachers, living most of their lives outside the law except when employed on casual labouring work. Their practice was never to go poaching together, so that if one was caught he could claim mistaken identity, since no one could tell the two apart. Nevertheless the law did catch up with them sometimes and both spent spells in prison. Their exploits caught the attention of Sir Edward Henry, who was experimenting with the use of fingerprints to identify individuals. With the help of identical twins, including the Foxes, he was able to prove his theory correct.

Poverty continued to haunt the working classes during the nineteenth century. In 1835 the Hitchin Union of Parishes was formed. This meant in practical terms that a new brick workhouse was built at Hitchin, to cope with the poor and aged of Hitchin, Stevenage, Baldock and surrounding villages, which each contributed to its upkeep from local rates and jointly appointed the Board of Guardians. Though this may have been a more efficient use of resources, it served to increase the dread of the workhouse, or 'the Union' as it came to be known, because it meant that those unfortunate enough to be sent there would now be cut off from familiar surroundings and from friends and neighbours. Once the new workhouse at Hitchin was built, the old one at the south end of Stevenage was no longer needed and it was closed.

There were some self-help groups which went some way towards insuring against hard times. In Stevenage, there was a Labourers' Friendly Society which met at the White Horse in 1823. Eleven years later the first meeting of the Stevenage Provident Society was held on 28 April 1834 and continued successfully into the next century. Its combined annual meeting and dinner, known as the Club Feast, was a lively event at which beer was plentiful. On one of these occasions a member was excluded for striking another on the head with a quart mug.

The very poor, who lived in insanitary cottages such as those in Back Lane, relied heavily on charity. The ladies of the parish combined lessons in hygiene and domestic economy with religious teaching by holding regular Mothers' Meetings. The worst times for the poor were the winter months, when there was no work on the land for the men. A hard winter brought much suffering. Miss Bailey Denton, of Orchard Court, was one who gave generously of her time and money, as recorded in the parish magazine for April 1888:

> Miss Bailey-Denton writes to inform us that the penny dinners she has provided during the winter months are now discontinued. She wishes to thank those ladies who have kindly assisted her at the dinners. Also Mrs James Smyth for her usual donation and Miss Barclay, Mrs Fellowes, Mrs Salmon and Dr Ward for their contributions.

Another Stevenage resident who regularly came to the aid of the poor was William Wurr, estate agent and church organist, whose name was synonymous with music in late nineteenth-century Stevenage. Every winter he gave 'coal concerts', extremely popular events which drew on talented amateurs to entertain the townspeople and to raise money to buy coal for the poor.

Poverty was a contributory factor to the high infant mortality rate in the town. Month after month the names of young babies were recorded in both the baptism and the burial registers. In September 1871, for example, Robert Parker was baptized on 3rd and buried on 13th and Harry Blow baptized on 22nd and buried on 30th. Interestingly, the latter was the son of unmarried parents, John Deards and Ann Maria Blow. Death also struck the children of wealthy parents and rather more publicity was given to their loss, as shown in the November 1882 parish magazine:

> It is with deep regret that we have to record the death of the Revd Lingen Seager's infant son – a regret which we know has been very generally and sincerely shared in. . . .

There were frequent complaints about the quality of the town's drinking-water. The poor had to make do with ponds, such as those in the High Street, at Fisher's Green, Walkern Road and the notorious one in Back Lane. However, the population was on the whole surprisingly healthy, according to reports from the Medical Officer of Health in the 1880s. Nevertheless, it was felt necessary to provide fresh drinking-water and in 1885 the first piped water was provided from a borehole at Rooks Nest, opposite the house where the future novelist E.M. Forster was living with his widowed mother. Another borehole was later opened at Broomin Green.

Some alarming cases of serious illness still occurred, however. As late as April 1872 the *Stevenage Parish Magazine* reported:

> The small pox has carried off rapidly and suddenly two of our poor inhabitants, whose miserable dwellings were likely enough to aggravate the virulence of the disease. It is to be wished that some measures could be taken either to remove these wretched tenements in which disease is propagated, or to render them less unfit for human habitation.

Fortunately effective 'due precautions' were taken and the outbreak was contained. Yet exactly ten years later the magazine told the story of the unfortunate Annie Sharp of Norton Green, who was in service to a Hitchin family when she was taken ill. After three days with a fever she was sent, by train and fly (a small horse-drawn vehicle), to the small cottage where she and her five brothers and sisters were crowded together. Dr Hill Smith diagnosed Scarlet Fever and arranged for her to be sent to the Stevenage cottage hospital at Sishes. All ended well, but the editor was justly indignant: 'We do not know whether this is a case of ignorance or of reckless and selfish carelessness; but we know the wonder is that in the face of such facts infectious diseases do not spread.'

In comparison with London, Stevenage was a haven of health and prosperity. In the 1880s the West Marylebone Committee of the Children's Country Holiday Home Scheme annually sent children to Stevenage for their summer holidays. Miss Eleanor Osborne Seager made the arrangements at the Stevenage end, finding local residents who were prepared to take in the children, meeting them at the station and dealing with problems which, by all accounts, were very few. The children were 'most liberally fed by the kind cottagers, many of whom became very fond of the children.' They were also 'much pleased to take 2 or 3 children for 5/- a week each.'

Even boys, whom some other places were 'strangely unwilling' to take, were welcome in Stevenage. The very few complaints of bad behaviour were not serious; one little boy of six was nicknamed 'Tiger' because of 'his great fighting propensities' and another was annoyed because 'he was not allowed to run round the garden in his night shirt at 3 o'clock in the morning.'

Stevenage children regularly sent flowers to children in London hospitals. In September 1887 the matron of the London Hospital in Whitechapel, wrote to the girls' Sunday school teachers:

> I have pleasure to acknowledge with many thanks your very acceptable gift of fruit and flowers. The children thoroughly appreciate them and they contribute very much to the bright and cheerful aspect that we are always desirous of maintaining in their wards. Cordially thanking you for your kind remembrance of our little ones.

The nineteenth century was notable for the development of modern forms of local government. Before the old parish vestry meetings were abolished, their increasing responsibilities were becoming too much to cope with under the old system. In April 1872 it was noted that Mr Elliott, for thirty years Master of the National School, was resigning from that office, but it was hoped that he would continue as Vestry Clerk, in which his knowledge of all the details of parochial business and his accuracy in the transaction of them are of great value. The labour both of mind and body which is now required to keep the parochial rate books in conformity with the rules of the Local Government Board, is very considerable. . . .

Among the old institutions which disappeared during this period of local government reform, were the turnpike trusts. After 1862 their functions were taken over by local highway boards. Other boards and committees were established, making it necessary for many towns to build new public halls· to accommodate local board meetings, magistrates' courts, official functions and also social events. A town hall was built in Railway Street (now Orchard Road) in Stevenage, in 1871, but

> The Town Hall is open but not opened. In other words, no ceremonial has yet been held sufficiently imposing to grace such an important event as the inauguration of our new public building. . . . We look forward to many pleasant winter evenings to be spent within its walls. The only suggestion we should make . . . is that a piece of pavement be laid down in front of each of the doors. Railway Street clay is not the pleasantest thing to alight on from a carriage.

The town hall rapidly became the accepted place for all manner of events. From June 1872 the Saturday straw plait market, previously held in the open space between Holy Trinity church and Southend Farm, was moved to the town hall and a small admittance fee charged. At that time there were often more than three hundred plait sellers at the market, who between them could take over £100 in sales, a considerable sum in those days.

There was ceaseless charitable activity in the town, often taking the form of public concerts and bazaars which not only raised money but also gave great pleasure to the participants and the audience. Some of these events required an enormous amount of time, hard work and expertise. The 1883 bazaar in aid of the fund for a new organ in the parish church is a typical example. Organized by a managing committee of Messrs Bates, Bennison, Draper, T. Ellis, M. Green, C.S. Toll, Wadsworth and Wurr, it ran for two weekdays and made a gross total of £440. Not surprisingly, it was 'hailed on all sides as a brilliant success.' In the days when most ordinary people did not often visit London, a bazaar such as this, with stalls draped in red and white, a gigantic shoe and a miniature well, ornately decorated and stocked with dolls and toys, must have been a good substitute for an Oxford Street department store. A further excitement was the opening ceremony performed by Lady Lytton of Knebworth, in the presence of 'a fashionable company'.

In the autumn of 1887 there were complaints about 'the intense cold' of the public hall and the hope was expressed that some steps would be taken to warm it properly before winter was quite set in, thereby earning the gratitude of the magistrates, the Local Board and 'all those who are attracted by entertainment and public meetings.'

Stevenage fair, by this time almost entirely a pleasure fair, continued to visit the High Street, as it had done since 1287. In 1821 its dates had been changed to 22 September and at the same time, Stevenage market-day was moved to a Wednesday. In 1887, exactly six hundred years after the granting of its charter,

> the annual Fair was held in the main street of Stevenage on September 22 and 23. The merry-go-rounds, swing-boats etc were well patronised and large crowds were drawn together by the well-known bargains to be obtained at the rival crockery stalls. The quiet order and general good behaviour of those attending the fair deserve more than a passing notice.

Queen Victoria's Golden Jubilee took place in 1887. Throughout the country plans were made to celebrate and to make some permanent memorial of the occasion. Stevenage excelled itself in the number of Jubilee projects it achieved. The fire brigade was supplied with splendid new uniforms and a new fire bell was erected by public subscription next to the White Lion in the High Street. Mr John Bailey Denton offered to give sufficient trees to plant on both sides of the High Street, from the Bowling Green to the Six Hills. After a little deliberation, this offer was accepted, a committee was set up to raise funds to plant and protect the trees and the Local Board agreed to become responsible for their future upkeep. Other committees and individuals undertook fundraising for the Women's Jubilee Offering and for the public celebrations.

A glowing report of the events of the Jubilee was given in the *Local Magazine*:

> The pretty High Street had been rendered still more attractive by the gay decorations of the householders on either side; noticeable amongst these were the residences of the Rev. G. Litting, Mr Franklin and Mr Wurr . . . on the left, just above

Middle Row, tables had been placed to seat over 900 people, the whole being covered in with an arrangement of tarpaulin, to meet sunshine or rain, open towards the houses and closed towards the street, a very necessary arrangement on a dusty day.

At ten o'clock the Bowling Green, at the head of the High Street (one of those greens which add so much to the beauty of our rural towns) was rendered full of life and colour by the arrival of numerous people and children in picturesque holiday attire. . . . At 10.15 the procession started, headed by a large banner bearing the words 'God save the Queen'. . . . Wending its way through the lovely avenue to the picturesque parish church (both of which, in beauty, the town may well be proud of) the procession arrived in good time for the thanksgiving service. . . . The crowded congregation heartily joined in the services, the singing led by a full choir, with Mr Wurr at the organ. . . . Then more than 900 adults sat down to a meal of beef, new potatoes, pickles, beer and plum pudding, set on tables tastefully decorated with flowers under the guidance of Mrs Fellowes. . . . Dinner being ended, the Fire Engine, well manned and well horsed, appeared in front of the new Jubilee Fire Bell. And S.P. Nash, Esq., the captain, having clashed its first signal summons, the Fire Brigade galloped off to the Bowling Green, where the National Anthem was sung by the whole parish.

The century drew to a close amid a small explosion of new building. In 1883 the Educational Supply Association (ESA) opened a factory near the station at the top of Julian's Road. In rapid succession a series of new roads was built to house the workers. Basil's Road, named after the son of the managing director, was one of the first. A cluster of roads near the ESA, off Fisher's Green Road, including Bournemouth, Southsea, Huntingdon and Jubilee Roads, became known as the 'New Town' and established their own football club, the Newtown Rovers.

Other, more substantial houses were built along the London Road, between south end and the Six Hills. The young E.M. Forster described them disparagingly as 'ugly new houses [which] much disfigured the road.' His ten childhood years at Rooks Nest House from 1883 to 1893 were, he later said, the happiest of his life. He never forgot his old home, the beauty of the surrounding countryside, the friendship of the Franklins at the farm next door, the Postons at Highfield or the companionship of the garden boys Wray, Bible, Field, Chalkley and Ansell.

Rooks Nest House, *c.* 1980, home of E.M. Forster, 1883–93, and of composer Elizabeth Poston, 1914–87.

The Twentieth Century to 1946

When the new century opened Stevenage parish covered an area of about 4,545 acres, of which, according to the Board of Agriculture, 3,200 acres were arable land, 916 acres permanent grass and 325 acres wood. These figures serve to emphasize that, although the population had increased to 3,957 (three times what it had been a century before), Stevenage was still predominantly a farming community. The High Street itself still contained a number of farmhouses and barns and there were many associated businesses, such as saddlers and blacksmiths. The south end of the town was very rural, with Southend Farm and Pound Farm almost next door to each other. Apart from the High Street and the roads newly built at the end of the previous century, the whole of the remaining parish acreage was rural.

Many improvements had been made to the town's amenities; piped water was available to many, footpaths beside roads were more often than not paved, gutters and drains kept the streets cleaner, public places, and some private homes, were lit by gas manufactured in the town at the old workhouse, which now became known as the Gas House. Yet there were still people in the early years of the century who suffered acute poverty. The tiny hamlets of Fisher's Green and Norton Green each contained cottages whose occupants, dependent on seasonal work on the land, had no reserves to fall back on in bad weather. Cut off from the rest of the town it was more difficult for them to take part in social events, a situation which the Church attempted to rectify through the Fisher's Green Mission, established in 1907 in a cottage formerly belonging to a Mr Davis. Here, services and Mothers' Meetings were held, a small library was set up and there were occasional outings, such as the one to the newly built Letchworth Garden City in June 1908. A similar, but smaller, mission was later set up at Norton Green.

There were other hamlets and outlying farms in the parish, including Bedwell, Broomin Green, Rooks Nest, Pin Green and

Opposite, above: a cricket team at Stebbing Farm, Fisher's Green, in 1910, with the farmhouse in the background; *below*: the Dave family outside the Three Horseshoes public house, Pin Green, *c*. 1910.

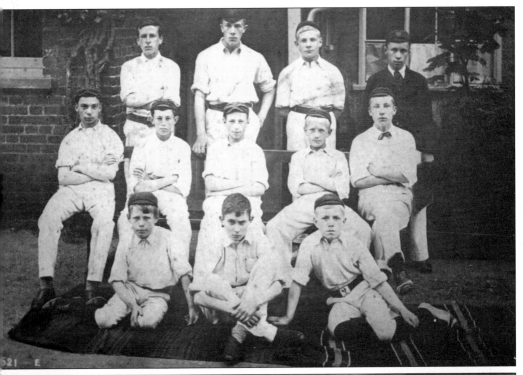

Highfield. The latter was a substantial country house, the home of the Poston family. Charles Poston took a close interest in the town and was a generous supporter of local causes. It was he who paid for a prefabricated meeting-hall, known as the Parish Room, to be erected at the top of Basil's Road in 1898, providing a convenient meeting-place for the people living in the recently built houses in this part of the town. He next turned his attention to the need for a working men's club in Stevenage, and was the driving force in achieving it. Plans were well in hand by October 1905, the month his daughter, Elizabeth, the future composer, was born. In December of that year the club was opened on the site of a farm in the High Street, between O'Clee's the butchers and the home of the Courbold-Ellises, later known as the Cromwell hotel.

As well as the immediate local needs, Stevenage people supported a great many charities. There were branches of the League of Pity, the Waifs and Strays Society, various missionary societies, the National Society for the Prevention of Cruelty to Children and the Band of Mercy, concerned with the care of animals, to name but a few. There may now be nostalgia for an age when vehicles were horse-drawn, but behind the picturesque scenes there was much suffering and cruelty. One young lady who took a very active role in the Band of Mercy was Dorothy Grosvenor, daughter of Dr A. Grosvenor, who was largely responsible for raising the funds to provide a drinking-trough at the Bowling Green for horses passing through the town.

The early twentieth century was a great time for florid advertisements in the press. The businesses in Stevenage High Street

Charles Poston, who lived at Highfield from 1886 until his death in 1913. A benefactor the town, he was also the model for the character of Charles Wilcox in E.M. Forster's *Howards End*. His daughter, Elizabeth, became a noted composer.

The stableyard behind O'Clee's butcher's shop, No 33 High Street, *c.* 1910–20. Harry O'Clee is standing far left.

9 High Street, 1975. For uch of this century the house as a doctor's surgery.

joined the fray with enthusiasm, even though it was admitted that in so small a town there was little point in advertising as everyone knew everyone else. Premises were not numbered – 'Fresson's Pharmacy, High Street', 'John Bond, Fruiterer & Greengrocer, Poulterer etc, High Street, Stevenage, Families waited upon daily', or 'F. Larkinson, High Street, Stevenage, China, Glass, Earthenware . . . ' was sufficient address.

Dentist F.S. Higgins, MPS, was one who believed in the value of publicity. His 1905 advertisements became ever more persuasive. Starting with his price-list for 'Gold-Medal Artificial Teeth . . . mounted on vulcanite . . 2/6, 3/6, 5/- per Tooth', he went on to extol the virtues of nitrous-oxide gas – 'Perfect purity of the Gas is guaranteed. . . The most nervous need not fear.' His next advertisement included a report of a speech from the Bishop of Newcastle:

> . . . of all the pains of the human body the one which attracted least sympathy from others was toothache. He had spent many hours in a Dentist's room, and could hardly look on one yet without a shudder. One of the happiest times of his life, all the same, was when he had all his teeth extracted, and he felt, if he had his time to live over again, he would rather have them all out at the beginning. He attributed a great deal of illness to bad teeth, because of improper digestion of food.

Stevenage continued to expand. In 1906 New Road was built by the Great Northern Railway Company. It was a wide, straight road, running parallel to the railway line, from Broomin Green, through Fairview Farm to the station, where it joined Fisher's Green Road. Subsequently its name was changed to Fairview Road, at the request of residents. For many years the only place to cross the railway line at the south end of the town was by means of an unmanned, uncontrolled, level crossing through the old brickyard (now Brick Kiln Road) to Trinity Road. A dreadful accident had occurred in 1886, when two children, on their way to school from Norton Green, had been killed by an express train as they attempted to cross the line in thick fog. Not until Chequers Bridge Road was built was there a safe crossing.

The expanding and increasingly literate population of the town was eager for knowledge. Each winter a series of lectures was given at the town hall, sometimes under the auspices of Cambridge University Extension lectures. Some of the lecturers were the leading authorities in their subjects, such as the nature photographer

The Syrinx Gas Company, 1883–8, which operated from premises in what is now Fairview Road.

Richard Kearton, sociologist Sidney Webb and author Percival Westell. Occasionally plans went awry. The Cambridge University Extension lectures for 1907 were to have been on 'The Age of Elizabeth' but at a late stage it was discovered that the lecturer, Mr R.F. Honter, had been double-booked. The committee was hastily summoned and agreed to fall back on their second choice of subject, 'The Republic of Florence'. The lecturer was a Mr E.M. Forster, promising novelist, who retained his links with his old friends, the Postons at Highfield and the Franklins at Rooks Nest Farm next door to his former home. His lectures, for which he received a fee of £30, were 'wonderfully successful' and the Popular Lecture Society made a profit of £6 10s. 7d.

Another young man with a bright future was William Jowitt, son of the rector, who achieved the 'brilliant success' of first class

estover, a private school, on corner of Hitchin Road and ian's Road, *c.* 1910.

honours in Jurisprudence at Oxford in 1906. No doubt this news cheered the rector, who had been unwell earlier in the year.

One of the preoccupations of the early twentieth century was the question of votes for women and no doubt Stevenage was as divided as the rest of the country on this subject. The attitude of the Bishop of St Albans, when he visited the town in February 1910 to talk on missionary work, must have caused no small irritation. The *Local Magazine* reported:

> His Lordship was asked, after acceding to the invitation, whether he preferred to address a congregation of men only, or one of men and women, and he has expressed a desire on this occasion to meet men only and to give the address in the Parish Room. . . .

Among local promoters of votes for women was Lady Constance Lytton of Knebworth, a leading member of the Women's Social and Political Union, who was imprisoned for her part in the London demonstrations of 1909 and 1910.

Modern technology was making its impact on Stevenage. A few people now had motor cars and drove through the High Street sending up clouds of dust from the unsurfaced road. Bicycles were more within the means of most people, although the curate and the district nurse both needed financial assistance to acquire theirs. The services of the district nurse were provided through a fund supported by voluntary contributions. Her address changed several times, from No. 148 High Street to No. 8 Essex Road and eventually, in 1916, to

No. 19 Julian's Road because 'No-one saw her brass plate in Essex Road [but] everybody passes along Julian's Road.' Incidentally, at this time the name Essex Road applied only to the first few houses, as far as the sharp left-hand bend. From there on, the road was originally known as Percy Avenue.

The widespread use of bicycles meant that accidents occurred from time to time and in 1910 the 'tragic death in a bicycle accident' of Howard Smith of Stanmore Road was reported. But bicycles were kept in their place and there was a very strict no cycling by-law in The Avenue, for example, as the public were reminded occasionally in the press. Another comparatively recent invention, the telephone, was fast becoming commonplace, as shops and businesses included telephone numbers in their advertisements.

The Health Centre, Stanmore Road, 1987. The centre stands on the site of the former police station and courthouse, whose weather vane has been retained on the new building.

Railway transport was in its heyday and work was going on to build a line from Hertford to Stevenage. In 1913 there were over three hundred and fifty workmen – known as Navvies – employed on this project, many of them living temporarily in Stevenage. It was anticipated that their numbers would increase to six hundred before the work was complete and a room in Albert Street was rented by the Navvy Mission Society, a national organization concerned for their welfare, to provide the men with a place to meet, read and relax.

In 1911 there were nationwide celebrations to mark the coronation of King George V and Queen Mary. Miss Mary Seager, of Orchard Cottage, was made local secretary for the Queen Mary Coronation Gift, which gave her the dubious privilege of asking all local residents named Mary, May, Maria, Marian or Miriam to contribute towards a gift for the new queen. Eighty-six of them did.

There was sadness during the early years of the century over a succession of deaths among men who had been prominent in the affairs of the town. In 1912 the death of Rector Jowitt, perhaps the best-known and best loved rector the town had ever had, left a great void and the feeling that an era had ended. Canon Molony, who succeeded him, had a difficult task. In 1913 another Stevenage personality, who had worked closely with Rector Jowitt, died. This was William Wurr, for many years organist at St Nicholas' and the town's leader in all things musical. His annual 'coal concert' to raise money for heating for the poor was just one example of his contribution to the town's life. However, as if to prove that no one is indispensable, a concert given two months after his funeral by sisters Ruth, Margery and Phyllis Eyre, was reported as 'the best concert ever heard in Stevenage.' Phyllis was the wife of Clarence Elliott, who established the famous nursery for alpine plants at Six Hills.

Nicholas' church, 1910.

A further blow to the community came in 1913 with the death of Charles Poston, whose generosity had helped provide many amenities. Shortly afterwards his widow and two young children moved from Highfield to Rooks Nest House, where twenty years previously the young E.M. Forster had lived. To continue the gloomy trend, in 1915 a prominent Methodist, Josiah Smart, died, 'A loss which the whole town of Stevenage felt . . . a public man of honest and straightforward worth.'

In 1914 the new rector, Canon Molony, having tried to carry out long overdue renovations to the huge old rectory, decided to sell it and build another, smaller, house further up Rectory Lane. He also set about the urgent task of restoration at St Nicholas' church where 'The rain has been streaming down the inside walls in the south-west corner of the transept and the boarding of the nave has required further temporary repairs in order to save people from going through the flooring.'

It seems that during 1913 and 1914 most people continued their usual activities oblivious of the threat of war. Local concerns included damage to the hay crop caused by children trespassing to pick buttercups; the great success of the annual flower show at which the number of exhibits was 'so large that they tended to squeeze out the visitors'; pride that the National Schools had at last achieved the report 'Attendance excellent'; a series of smoking concerts in the town hall, publicized as promoting harmony. But possibly the establishment of a Stevenage branch of the Navy

League, whose purpose was to send boys to sea, was a response to the increasingly tense international situation.

When war was announced in August 1914, its effects were quickly felt. There was no conscription initially but many local men volunteered for active service and some were sent abroad immediately. Within a month two of them, Henry Forder and Eric Guinness, were wounded, though not seriously. Voluntary organizations came swiftly into being. The Stevenage Local Relief Fund (Hon. Sec. Mr T. Seager Berry) and the Soldiers' and Sailors' Families Association (Treasurer, Lady Fellowes) existed primarily to raise money to help the dependants of servicemen, while another, led by Mrs Heathcote, knitted garments for the soldiers themselves. A War Workers' Department was set up at the Grange, where volunteers made bandages and dressings for use on the battlefields.

Letters from the war zone were initially cheerful and confident, often referring gratefully to supplies sent from home, as one officer wrote, 'The parcel has arrived from Mrs Grosvenor and I have dished out the woollies to the men.' Later, letters were often more sombre; several Stevenage soldiers wrote in 1915 about their experience on the battlefield, where they were saved by the Angel of Mons.

As the war continued, shortages and restrictions became commonplace in England. In December 1915 the Home Office issued a Lighting Order for the county of Hertford, requiring buildings to be blacked out after dark, to prevent stray light giving guidance to enemy aircraft, those new and terrifying vehicles of destruction. Some bombs were dropped over Stevenage, destroying barns in Bedwell Lane. Canon Molony, after a frustrating attempt to hang black-out curtains over the west window of Holy Trinity church, remarked wryly on the famine of curtain rings in the town. As regards food, there was no famine in a country district like Stevenage, where many people could grow their own food, but there were shortages of certain produce and people were asked to consume less, on a voluntary basis. There were also increasing difficulties in obtaining paper and other essential supplies.

As more men went into the armed forces their jobs were taken over by women, many of whom were drafted into the Land Army to do necessary farm work. Others worked for the railway company, or in shops and offices where previously staff had been entirely male. The First World War brought immense suffering. The death toll was dreadful, but so too was the ordeal of men who were gassed, physically injured or afflicted with shell-shock. For those who waited at home there were long silences when they did not know if

e War Memorial, erected
'21.

their loved ones were alive or dead. If wounded men were sent back to England, they were not necessarily within reach of their families. For a time there was a VAD (Voluntary Aid Detachment, Nursing Service) Hospital at Bragbury End, which was moved in 1917 to Knebworth Golf Club House, but not all Stevenage men were placed so close to home. Some were taken to the hospital at Rickmansworth, a very difficult place to get to by the limited public transport available, and others were sent even further afield.

Eventually the war came to an end, but life could never be as it was before 1914. The long list of Stevenage men who lost their lives was inscribed on a gleaming white war memorial erected on the Bowling Green in 1921.

In 1927 a new small factory, the Stevenage Knitting Company, opened in Sish Lane, offering welcome employment opportunities for women. By this time Stevenage also boasted its own cinema, the

he Publix Cinema on the
owling Green, *c.* 1920.

Stevenage tradesmen's outing
1920s. Back row, left to right:
Jack 'Nonox' (?) Shepherd,
Walt Piggott, 'Len' Game,
'Bert' Aldrige, Chris Tompso
'Bill' Jellis, 'Bob' Field,
Herbert A. Stutley. Front row:
'Jack' Lindsey, 'Bob' Gray,
'Cutie' Buckingham, George
Tompson.

Publix, at the top of the Bowling Green. Other leisure activities included outings in Mr Candler's North Star motor coach, which he had named after the former public house of the same name. Since 1920 this building, No. 12 High Street, had been the Stevenage office of solicitor William Brignall, later Brignall, White and Orchard.

In the 1930s unemployment was a continuing problem throughout the country. The Jarrow March was one of the most memorable events of the time, designed to draw attention to the plight of out-of-work men from the former shipbuilding town in Durham. Led by MP Ellen Wilkinson, the marchers walked the whole distance to the Houses of Parliament in London. As they passed through Stevenage they were given food and rest. One marcher subsequently made his home in the town.

Following the Housing Acts of 1919 and 1924, the Stevenage Urban District Council was empowered to build houses to let to local people living in substandard accommodation. Haycroft Road, Whitesmead Road, Longcroft Road, Ellis Avenue and Lawrance Avenue were the first of these. The latter two roads were named after two respected and long-serving members of the Council, T.W. Ellis and T. Lawrance.

North Star public house, now
Nos. 10–12 High Street.
(Painting by H. Roberts,
1910.)

A. Putnam's Boot-and-
Shoe-maker's premises on the
corner of Stanmore Road and
Church Lane, 1925.

However, there still many people living in homes without modern
facilities and the Public Baths, or 'Slipper Baths', next to the
almshouses in Church Lane provided a valuable service. The Urban
District Council's Accounts for the year ending 31 March 1935 show
that the annual cost of running the baths was £54 4s. 4d.,
while income from admission charges and use of towels totalled
£23 14s. 1d.

In 1935 there were celebrations to mark the Silver Jubilee of King
George V and Queen Mary. The third section of The Avenue – to be
known as the Jubilee Avenue – was planted with horse chestnut and
lime trees, along a path which deviated slightly from the original.
J. Marston Popple, former chairman of the Urban District Council,
gave land to provide a public playing field adjoining the Stevenage
Cricket Club ground, to be known as the King George V Playing
Fields. At this time too, the Urban District Council planned to build
a public swimming pool and had earmarked a site, but as things
turned out, the plan did not come to fruition.

In 1937 a young man named Philip Ireton was elected to the
Urban District Council, representing the Labour Party, which he had
joined at the age of fourteen. He had been born in 1904, in Walkern
Road, into a family which had lived in Stevenage for several
generations and he had ideas for the future of the town.

By 1938 it was clear that war was once again imminent. Mindful
of the horrors of poison gas in the First World War, the authorities
began issuing gas masks to the entire population, including infants,

Broadwater village, 1931. Left
to right: Ronnie Pea, Margaret
Cain, Lottie Moss, Peggy
Dickson.

who had to be totally enclosed in a protective apparatus. There was then a brief period of respite until, on 3 September 1939, the Second World War began.

The dreaded gas attacks did not materialize, but it was only too clear that aeroplanes, by now more advanced and numerous than in 1914, would be used extensively to drop bombs. Strict black-out regulations were immediately enforced after dark and no street lights, uncurtained windows or vehicle headlights were allowed. White lines were painted round trees and other objects in the hope of making them more visible to pedestrians and vehicles after dark. It was only too obvious to everyone that Stevenage, so close to London and on the Great Northern Railway line, would be in danger. Underground air-raid shelters were built in school playgrounds, at the south end of Church Lane and in other roads. Some residents built their own shelters in their gardens, but the majority had no special precautions apart from taking cover when the air-raid warning sounded. The signal was given by a siren standing in the fire brigade yard on the corner of Basil's Road and its dismal wailing could be heard all over the town.

Many Stevenage men were called up to serve in the armed forces. Women were required to work in factories, such as the ESA, where they made ammunition boxes and helped with the construction of the wooden Mosquito aircraft, or on the land once again, as part of the Land Army. Some women were also conscripted into the WRNS, WRAF, ATS or other services.

At Rooks Nest House Elizabeth Poston, who was beginning to make her name as a composer, received a summons to work for the BBC. This she did for the duration of the war, based variously in London, Bedford and Bristol. For much of her time she had the task of sending coded messages via recorded music to occupied countries in Europe, a frightening responsibility when any mistake could have brought disaster to the resistance movements she was contacting. The war also brought about a reunion with E.M. Forster, now an internationally famous novelist, who had lived at Rooks Nest House as a child. In 1910 his novel, *Howard's End* had been published. In the book he had included memories of his old home and had used Elizabeth Poston's parents as prototypes for his characters Charles and Ruth Wilcox and was justifiably a little nervous of meeting Mrs Poston. However, he was persuaded to revisit Rooks Nest and a friendship was established which lasted for the rest of his life.

One casualty of the war was Stevenage fair, whose colourful lights and noise could not be permitted. Stevenage people were determined

An ARP exercise on 24
February 1940 in the Basil's
Road First Aid Post.

A candlelit party held at the
Town Hall in 1945, for the
volunteers who had worked at
the Old Castle canteen during
the Second World War.

that a tradition of nearly seven hundred years should not die and a single stall was put up in the High Street every 22 and 23 September for the duration of the war, to ensure the continuity of the charter of 1281. In order to cheer up the war workers who were billeted in Stevenage a social club, later known as the Lytton Club, was built in a field in Pound Avenue.

Those men who were too old or too young to be called up, or who were in reserved occupations, joined the Home Guard, the unpaid amateur force which protected towns and villages throughout the country and which would resist the Germans if they invaded. Many of these men already worked long hours in arduous daytime occupations. Some of them travelled daily on crowded, blacked-out trains, to work in bomb-scarred London and were mentally and physically tired even before they gave up evenings and weekends to Home Guard training. ARP (Air Raid Precautions) wardens also had onerous responsibilities. They were the people who watched day and night for signs of enemy aircraft and alerted residents to possible dangers from lighted windows. Women joined voluntary organizations and many were involved in running the canteen for troops at the Old Castle Inn in the High Street.

The Stevenage Fire Brigade, with other local brigades, helped to put out the fires caused by incendiary bombs in London and other

big towns. When the City of London was in flames, the red glow from the fire could be seen in the night sky by anxious Stevenage people. About five hundred London children were sent to Stevenage as evacuees, living in the homes of local families and often becoming life-long friends. A few never did go back to the city.

When Victory in Europe was announced in 1945, the whole population of Stevenage seemed to erupt into the High Street. There were people everywhere that night, just walking about, complete strangers talking to each other as if they were bosom friends, the air thick with emotion.

Once the war was over, there was much to do before normal life could be resumed. The rolls of barbed wire in The Avenue were eventually removed and tanks and army lorries ceased churning up the Bury Mead. Lights came on again and air-raid shelters were closed off, but food rationing remained. However, great efforts were made to provide jellies and cakes for the children's celebration parties that were organized all over the town, some outdoors, such as the street party in Albert Street, others in the Nissen hut in Sish Lane, the town hall and in private houses. At last, people could begin to live again.

CHAPTER EIGHT

New Stevenage

Hardly had the victory celebrations after the Second World War died down and a return to normality begun, when the government announced that part of its plan for post-war reconstruction was the building of a ring of satellite towns round London. Stevenage would be the first. The news came as a shock, although discussions about ways of rehousing people from the slums of big cities had, in fact, been taking place for many years. Sir Patrick Abercrombie's *Greater London Plan*, published in 1944, had specifically mentioned building 'new towns' on a radius of about 30 miles round London. Even earlier than that, people inspired by Sir Ebenezer Howard's book *Garden Cities of Tomorrow* and by the founding of Letchworth Garden City in 1903 had been promoting the garden city movement.

One man who believed strongly in this approach was Councillor Philip Ireton. He was impressed by the Letchworth development and hoped to see something like it repeated in Stevenage. He saw such a development as a means both to bring more employment to the town and to help London's homeless, having been made aware of their plight as a member of the Town and Country Planning Association. When the satellite town proposals were drawn up at the end of the war, Knebworth had been suggested as one site. Philip Ireton pointed out that it did not have an alternative railway line, as Stevenage did with the Hertford loop, and that for this and other reasons, Stevenage would be more suitable. His voice was heeded.

Many local people were against the proposal to build a new town in Stevenage, however. There were fears that homes would be destroyed, that those who worked on the land (and there were many) would have their livelihoods taken away, and there was sorrow at the inevitable destruction of the countryside. Most people felt torn; they wanted to help the homeless, as indeed they had done during the war by taking evacuees from London, but they were frightened by the immensity of the change which was overtaking them.

One voice which was heard nationwide was that of E.M. Forster, then living in Cambridge but still in close touch with his old friends in Stevenage. As a Socialist himself and a generous friend to those in need, he understood only too well the dilemma. In a radio broadcast in 1946, he said:

> People must have houses. They must, and I think of working class friends in north London who have to bring up four children in two rooms . . . but I cannot equate the problem. It is a collision of loyalties. I cannot free myself from the conviction that something irreplaceable has been destroyed, and that a little piece of England has died as surely as if a bomb had hit it.

William Jowitt, the brilliantly clever son of the former rector, who had been ennobled with the title Lord Jowitt of Stevenage and appointed Lord Chancellor of England in 1945, was instrumental in helping to bring about the Town and Country Planning Act which allowed for the establishment of new towns. Thus, by a strange coincidence, two men who had known each other as boys in Stevenage, both from privileged backgrounds, both espousing the Socialist cause, became involved in the debate about the future of their childhood home, but from opposite sides.

Children at St Nicholas' School (formerly known as the National Schools), Bury Mead 17 October 1958.

It is important to realize the scale of the changes that Stevenage was facing. Its population was six thousand in 1946 and the plan was to increase it to sixty thousand when the new town was complete. It is interesting to compare these figures with other new towns designated shortly afterwards. Between 1951 and 1971 the population of Stevenage rose from 7,168 to 67,080. In the same period Hemel Hempstead's population increased from 23,437 to 70,380, Welwyn Garden City's from 18,804 to 40,450 and Hatfield's from 9,256 to 25,360. Of all the designated new towns, Stevenage was not only the smallest to start with, but it experienced the biggest growth of 1,000 per cent as opposed to 300 per cent for Hemel Hempstead, 220 per cent for Welwyn and 250 per cent for Hatfield. Stevenage was also the first, and therefore more likely to suffer from early mistakes.

In 1946 Lewis Silkin, Minister of Town and Country Planning, came to Stevenage to address a public meeting of residents. When he arrived at the station he found that the name board had been covered up and 'Silkingrad' placed over it. Outside the town hall, Orchard Road was thronged with people who could not get in. Silkin was given a generally hostile reception, and, far from allaying fears, added annoyance to anxiety by telling people, 'You will have a new town whether you like it or not.' Stevenage became national news and made headlines in the papers.

Opponents of the new town were led by William Vernon Franklin of Rooks Nest Farm, Michael Tetley of the Priory and George Hearn of Corey's Mount. They appealed to the High Court against the decision, their case resting heavily on the argument that the result of the Enquiry was a foregone conclusion, as the Minister had made up his mind before hearing objections. There was jubilation when Mr Justice Henn Collins, in the King's Bench Division, upheld their appeal on the grounds that Mr Silkin may not have been an unbiased judge. However, this decision was overturned in the House of Lords on 25 July 1947, and the designation order became law.

The first Stevenage Development Corporation Board had already been nominated by Silkin and was now made public. The chairman was Clough Williams-Ellis and the sole representative from Stevenage was Councillor Philip Ireton. Even at this early stage there was the beginning of antipathy between the Development Corporation and the Urban District Council, whose views were not considered. The building of the new town began and the fears of residents were realized as the houses in Bedwell Lane and London Road, among others, were destroyed to make way for the planned new town. There had been some amendments to the original plan and promises had been made that the old town – by which the planners meant the High Street – would not be touched. But historically Stevenage was essentially a small country town, its farms and fields inseparable from its High Street commerce.

As the new town grew it attracted attention from all over the world. Its unique features included a system of cycle tracks beside roads, an idea pioneered by Chief Engineer Eric Claxton, with the intention of encouraging cyclists by separating them safely from motor vehicles. Pedestrian underpasses and a pedestrian town centre were other points of interest for visitors, as was the use of roundabouts instead of traffic lights, another of Eric Claxton's schemes.

For the first settlers in the new town, life was vastly different from that which they had left behind. Many families who had previously shared with in-laws now had a house and garden of their own for the first time. Others were glad to move from old, poor standard accommodation to modern homes with electricity and running water. But there was also evidence of culture shock and the 'New Town Blues', which sociologists seized upon as material for many a learned article. In these early days there were houses but little else; no shops, no places of entertainment, none of the amenities of urban life for the newcomers, who had perforce to make their way on foot or by bus to the old town High Street. Here shops such as O.P.

The Stevenage Branch of the Hertfordshire County Library next to the Town Hall in Orchard Road, 1959.

Thurlow, draper, and Cuthbert, grocer, on opposite corners of Albert Street, were regularly inundated with shoppers on Saturday mornings. Old town residents were bemused by the influx, particularly since the buses to Hitchin, the traditional shopping centre for north Hertfordshire, were now so full on market-days, Tuesdays and Saturdays, that they were unable to board.

For many newcomers, their clearest memory of the early days in Stevenage was of the mud around the sparkling new homes; they were, after all, living on a building site. As for the old town dwellers, however much they tried to welcome their new neighbours, through the churches especially, they could not help but be sad as another meadow, another hedgerow, another cottage, crumbled under the bulldozers. Woods where children were accustomed to play, were fouled by workmen; desecration seemed all about. Yet the new and old communities lived together remarkably well, perhaps because most of those who could not face the future in a changed Stevenage moved out and others made strenuous efforts to help the newcomers settle in. Many new town residents took up the challenge of building a new community with energy and commitment. Huw and Connie Rees, who themselves contributed immensely to the developing town, published a book entitled *The History Makers*, which describes the experiences of many of the pioneering new Stevenage residents.

It must be said also, that for some years there were divisions in the governance of the town, such as two separate housing lists, one held by the Development Corporation and the other by the Urban District Council. Nor was it quite in accord with the ethos of the new town movement that, as far as is known, none of the architects or planners deigned to live in the new houses and flats for which they were responsible.

The new town is divided into neighbourhoods, the intention being to give each the sense of a small community, with its own shops, church, public house and communal meeting-place, to complement the central facilities which may be a bus ride away. The historian Lionel Munby commented in 1974 that in Stevenage,

> roads provide a skeleton. They not only divide neighbourhood units but bind them together, conducting people from their homes to the town shopping centre and the factory area. . . . The roads also provide fingers of green in the urban landscape.

The neighbourhoods of Stevenage are based on ancient settlements, such as Chells, Pin Green, Symond's Green, Broadwater and Shephall. Before 1946, Shephall was a small village some 2½ miles from Stevenage. A walk across the field paths to Shephall was a pleasant afternoon excursion. Conversely, Shephall villagers would often walk or cycle into Stevenage for their shopping, or a visit to the cinema or, once a year, to the fair. In her book *Tyme out of Mind* Mary Spicer recalls these occasions:

> People came to the fair from miles around and there would be greetings and meetings with relations and friends. As there would be a long wait for buses we walked home across the fields, the sleeping cattle hardly stirring as we passed.

Shephall's church of St Mary dates from the twelfth century or possibly earlier. One of its bells is believed to be the oldest in Hertfordshire, cast in the late twelfth century. Opposite the church, across the lane, stands the Red Lion Inn, part of which is of fifteenth-century origin and around the village green still stand a number of sixteenth- and seventeenth-century cottages and the Jubilee Oak, which was planted in 1935 to commemorate the Silver Jubilee of King George V and Queen Mary. Although so close to Stevenage, Shephall had developed entirely separately, having been administered, since the Middle Ages, from St Albans as a detached part of the Hundred of Cashio, unlike the rest of the district which was within the Hundred of Broadwater. Shephalbury, or Shephall manor as it came to be called, belonged to the Nodes family during the sixteenth and seventeenth centuries and to the Heathcotes during the nineteenth century. In 1865 Mr Unwin Unwin-Heathcote demolished the earlier bury and built an immense Gothic mansion in its place. The last Heathcote to live there died in 1912, after which the house was let before finally being sold in 1939. During the Second World War it was used as a Polish training school.

The building of the Shephall neighbourhood of the new town took place between 1954 and 1959. The nucleus of the village around its ancient green was preserved, as was the manor, although divided from the rest by Broadhall Way. Other old buildings, and some not so old, were demolished; Half Hyde Farmhouse, the village school, the council houses and the rectory. As new roads were put in their place many were given derivatives of the old names, such as Oakfields, Peartree Way, Ridlin's End, Hadwell Close, Medalls Link, Half Hyde and Sleaps Hyde. Former Shephall rectors have their names perpetuated in Barnwell, Leslie Close, MacKenzie Square and Rudd Close and the old lords of the manor are remembered in Heathcote School and Nodes Drive.

industrial landscape.
gyle Way, seen from
equers Bridge Road, 1993.

Another feature of the new town which attracted visiting planners was the factory area. From the start, the concept of separation of residential and industrial roads was central to town planning. The disease and discomfort which characterized so many unplanned cities, where people were forced to breathe polluted air and live beside dangerous manufacturing processes, were in the forefront of many minds. To avoid this juxtaposition, the Stevenage industrial area was developed to the west of the railway line, with easy access to it and to the A1(M) by-pass, opened in 1961. To a great extent this plan harmonized with the existing pattern of life, as the railway had formed an effective boundary to much of the old town. The industrial area with its wide roads, sweeping grass verges and entirely functional buildings comprises some of the most successful new town architecture and design. On winter afternoons, when lights blaze from factory windows, it is quite spectacular.

The first road to be built in the industrial area was Argyle Way, named after the existing works of the Geo. W. King Company, which the Development Corporation had encouraged, controversially, to move to Stevenage from Hitchin in 1949. Some of the first companies to follow were Hawker-Siddeley Dynamics in 1952, Imperial Chemical Industries (ICI) and Pye Ether in 1953. In the same year the predecessor of Marconi Instruments, the old town electronics firm of WH Saunders, moved from its small premises in Bedwell Lane to one of the new factories. International Computers Ltd (ICL), Kodak, Bowater Packaging, British Aircraft Corporation (formerly English Electric) and Mentmore Manufacturing were among the larger firms which followed in the late 1950s. Hawker-Siddeley Dynamics and British Aircraft Corporation subsequently became part of a series of mergers which produced the giant British Aerospace (BAe), the town's major employer, which also sent large

Geo. W. King's factory, Argyle Way.

numbers of apprentices to Stevenage College every year. Meanwhile, in the old town the ESA and the Stevenage Knitting Company continued to employ local labour, but the world famous Vincent HRD motor bicycle company closed down.

The other major artery of the industrial area, Gunnel's Wood Road, took its title from a fourteenth-century field name, which had itself been named after a Scandinavian woman, possible a Dane of the time of the Viking raids. At the junction of these two great roads, Argyle Way and Gunnel's Wood Road, surrounded by swirling traffic, is the timber-framed sixteenth-century Broomin Green Farm, a lone survivor from the past. It was the birthplace, on 15 November 1590, of Richard Norwood, who grew up to become a sailor and a surveyor. He was the first to chart the Bermuda Islands, where he eventually settled with his family. He almost certainly went to the Petits' School on Burymead, but moved away with his family when he was ten and was unable to complete his education. Obviously a very clever boy, he must have received a good grounding at Stevenage because his surveying skills were entirely self-taught from books and his own experiments. In his old age he reflected on his childhood 'at Stevenage in Hertfordshire which I reckon among the many favours of God towards me.'

In 1737, at a time when those who wished to practise a non-conformist religion were required to register their places of worship, a certificate was issued to a group of Quakers, allowing them to use

ɔomin Green Farm, *c.* 1900.

Broomin Green Farm for worship. At some time before 1900 the external walls of the house were plastered over, so that the timber framing was protected from the weather. During the Second World War Broomin Green had the distinction of receiving the first German bombs to fall on Stevenage. Having survived this, the house was bought and renovated by Camford Engineering for use by directors for business meetings. Since Camford made car components, their

oomin Green Farm, *c.* 1980.

visitors included senior personnel from most of the major motor vehicle manufacturers.

The house is also reputed to have a ghost. Such claims were dismissed by the Hooper family who lived there during the late 1970s, when Mrs Hooper was the resident houekeeper. They ignored the odd way in which doorbells would ring, apparently of their own accord, but one summer's day the son of the family and a friend, two stalwart young men, heard footsteps upstairs. There were two flights of stairs which met on a landing and the two men ran up separately, to meet in the middle. There was no one else there. Only, there was a bricked-up doorway at one end of the landing and it was towards this that they heard the footsteps moving.

The building of the new town was subject to delays and frustrations, sometimes related to tensions between the Development Corporation and the Urban District Council, which in turn were often the result of changes in policy as Conservative and Labour

An aerial view of Stevenage, 1950–60. Franklin's Road is under construction in the foreground.

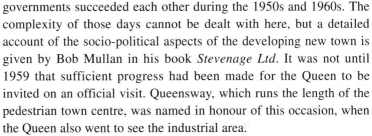

The Queen inspecting a rocket called *English Electric Thunderbird* at Gunnels Wood Road, 1959.

Philip Ireton, CBE, first Labour Chairman of Hertfordshire County Council, and first Freeman of the Borough of Stevenage.

governments succeeded each other during the 1950s and 1960s. The complexity of those days cannot be dealt with here, but a detailed account of the socio-political aspects of the developing new town is given by Bob Mullan in his book *Stevenage Ltd*. It was not until 1959 that sufficient progress had been made for the Queen to be invited on an official visit. Queensway, which runs the length of the pedestrian town centre, was named in honour of this occasion, when the Queen also went to see the industrial area.

Throughout these difficult years, one man who refused to lose his original vision and who gained the respect of all parties, was Philip Ireton. In addition to his responsibilities in Stevenage, he represented the town on the Hertfordshire County Council, for many years as leader of the Labour opposition. Always interested in education, he became a member of the County Education Committee in 1942 and was subsequently Chairman of Governors of a number of Stevenage schools and of the College of Further Education. As well as these and many other duties, he was also a Justice of the Peace, serving in the Stevenage Magistrates' Court for many years. Throughout all this political activity he did not forget his early lessons in horticulture at Letchmore Road School. Gardening remained important to him, something which he encouraged others to pursue through the Stevenage Allotment and Gardeners' Association and the Stevenage Horticultural Society. Most importantly, he did all in his power to help individuals in need.

The Sunday school party,
Parish Room, Basil's Road,
c. 1960. Top left, Revd Haro
Jones (standing); top right,
Revd Eric Gaskell (with pipe

All concerned with the new town realized that it was essential to provide centres for people to meet, to help the growth of a sense of community. The various religious denominations worked with the Development Corporation to build new churches in each neighbourhood. One very successful church, dedicated to St Andrew, grew up in a dual purpose building in Bedwell Crescent. It was led by the Revd Ted Harper, who created a vibrant congregation made up of old and young, newcomers and old town people. Ironically, it was not allowed to survive. The Development Corporation and St Albans Diocese between them agreed to build a large church in the town centre almost within a stone's throw of St Andrews, which it would replace.

The new church would also become the parish church for Stevenage, and all others, including the twelfth-century St Nicholas' and St Mary's churches and the nineteenth-century Holy Trinity, would become 'daughter' churches as part of a team ministry. By this plan the religious and civic authorities managed to upset a good many Anglicans throughout Stevenage, which perhaps had the merit

design for the new parish
rch of St George, 1956.

of uniting them. On 14 July 1956 a crowd gathered in a muddy field
to watch Queen Elizabeth the Queen Mother lay the foundation
stone of St George's church. The commemorative booklet stated, 'In
building St George's we are providing the heart of the parish.' In
November 1960 the Queen Mother returned for the consecration of
the new church, a spectacular event attended by choirs and
congregations from all over the town.

Meanwhile Methodist churches were being built at Broadwater
and Chells, a United Reformed church and a Friends' Meeting
House in Cutty's Lane, a Baptist church in Hydean Way and St
Joseph's Roman Catholic church in Bedwell Crescent, as well as
many others. Often the most successful church communities were
those which started in private houses or in temporary
accommodation, such as the two converted garages which served the
neighbourhood of Pin Green under the name of St Francis's church
in the 1950s and 1960s. The fellowship engendered in these years
paved the way for one of the first experiments in shared church
building, at a time when the ecumenical movement was in its
infancy. The change of name to All Saints, when the Oval church
and community centre was opened, reflects its shared use by
Anglicans, Roman Catholics and Methodists.

The first public houses to be built in the new town included Our Mutual Friend in Broadwater, a replacement for the original in London Road, the Twin Foxes in Rockingham Way, which recalls the poaching exploits of Albert and Ebenezer Fox, and the Peartree in Valley Way, its name taken from the ancient Peartree Wood. In the town centre itself the Longship follows the Danish theme based on naming the main through road Danestrete after the Danes Road mentioned in an early charter.

As the town centre grew it began to offer the leisure and shopping facilities for which people had previously flocked to the old town, while in each neighbourhood community centres provided meeting-places for residents in the immediate locality. Clubs and interest groups too numerous to list sprang up across the town as they continue to do today. Of those societies, which attracted membership from all parts of the town, the Lytton Players and the Stevenage Musical Society, both founded in the 1940s, are still flourishing today, the latter often

Stevenage Musical Society performing at St Nicholas' church, 1950. Peter Boorman is conducting.

rk beginning on Fairlands
ley lakes, 1971. Cllr. James
d is aloft.

bus shelters in the town
tre, November 1993.

performing in St George's church (recently renamed St Andrew and St George), which has proved a splendid concert hall, as well as housing the Stevenage Museum in its undercroft.

Many people were attracted to Stevenage in the belief that it would provide the best of both worlds; town facilities and access to the countryside. During the 1950s and 1960s, despite the continuous development going on around them, the majority of residents were very close to open country. As building increased and the population approached the planned sixty thousand, the Development Corporation began to talk of expansion. In 1966 it published a 'Master Plan', which included proposals to extend the designated new town area and to build a new road, known as 'Road 9', which would bisect and disrupt Fairlands Valley, an open tract of land within the town boundaries, which had become very dear to residents.

A protest group, the Stevenage Valley Association, was set up with the aim of preventing the building of Road 9, and it rallied considerable support. It handed in a petition of over twelve thousand signatures, and thoroughly publicized its case locally and in the national press. Despite this, it was able to make little impression on the Development Corporation and Ken Poole, librarian of Stevenage College and a founder of the Stevenage Valley Association, said at a public meeting on 17 April 1972, 'There seems to be some belief on their [the SDC's] part that the fact that they are experts means that the people who are not experts but who are acquainted with the problem, somehow are necessarily talking through their hats.' Subsequently the plans for Road 9 were shelved and finally dropped altogether. Fairlands Valley Park became one of the unique features of Stevenage, with its acres of public open space, adjoining woodland and its artificial sailing lakes.

The desire for expansion remained, however. In 1973 the Development Corporation put forward further proposals which would involve designating as development land extensive areas on the west of the Stevenage boundary and somewhat smaller areas on the east and north. There was very strong opposition, both from the surrounding villages which united under the Campaign Against Stevenage Expansion (CASE) and from within the existing town where the Stevenage Valley Association and the Campaign Against Unnecessary Stevenage Expansion (CAUSE) were active. Some people were particularly concerned for the countryside immediately to the north of the Stevenage boundary, known for its historical and literary associations as the Forster Country. A letter to *The Times*, dated 29 April 1976, was signed by thirty scholars from four continents and began, 'Our particular concern is the threat to an

95

exceptionally beautiful pocket of countryside which is also part of Britain's cultural heritage.' The Urban District Council was also against the expansion proposals. Following the subsequent Public Inquiry, the Inspector's decision, announced in 1978, was that the proposed expansion of Stevenage would not be allowed.

During this period there was increasing pressure from the town's elected council that it, without the Development Corporation, should have full control of the affairs of Stevenage. The life of the Development Corporation had been extended several times, but it was eventually wound up in 1980 and after a short transition period the government of the town was handed over to the local council, which now had borough status.

The Borough Council itself proposed, and was granted approval for, the extension of the Stevenage boundaries to take in land to the north-east of the town, known as Chells Manor and Wellfield Wood. There has also been pressure from private developers and one contentious area has continued to be the Forster Country. In 1989 a group known as the Friends of the Forster Country was established with the aim 'To preserve for all time the open green space to the north of Stevenage, part of which is known as the Forster Country.'

In the forty-seven years since it was designated a new town, Stevenage has seen more rapid change than at any time in previous centuries. But the real history of Stevenage is not about buildings, but about people, be they sixteenth-century haberdashers, eighteenth-century innkeepers or twentieth-century information technologists. As the motto on the borough coat of arms so aptly states, 'The heart of a town is in its people'.

Nellie Manning selling poppies for the Royal British Legion outside the Waitrose store, November 1993. The supermarket is on the corner Draper's Way, formerly occupied by first Green's, the Henderson's draper's shops. Mrs Manning is from an old Stevenage family. Her grandmother helped keep Stevenage Fair alive during t Second World War by holdin a stall in the High Street.

A garden party at Rooks Nest House to launch the Friends of the Forster Country, 21 May 1989.

Walking Tour

The walk follows the route of the old Great North Road from the Six Hills, through the High Street to the Bowling Green, then up The Avenue to St Nicholas church and along the Weston Road to Rooks Nest. A number of short diversions can be made, as described in the text.

> **Start on the west side of the Six Hills, where the old Great North Road is now a pedestrian way, leading to the Six Hills Way underpass. Spend a little time reading the information board here.**

The starting point for a walk through Stevenage's history is the same today as it has been for nearly two thousand years; the Six Hills beside the old main road. It is difficult now to visualize the way it used to be, the straight road running through wooded farmland, with the Six Hills on its east side. A remnant of the old road still exists here, as a sad little byway beside the entrance to industrial buildings.

From 1907 to 1954 a great attraction for gardeners was the Six Hills Nursery, owned by the internationally renowned plantsman Clarence Elliott. Specializing in alpine plants, the nursery attracted visitors from all over the country and also from abroad. Today the name lives on in a number of varieties developed by Clarence Elliott, such as the Six Hills Giant lavender. All that remains of the nursery is the beech avenue in the grounds of the North Hertfordshire College (formerly Stevenage College of Further Education).

Built as part of Hertfordshire County Council's forward-looking plan for a network of further education establishments, Stevenage College was fortunate in its first Principal, George Lighton. His dedication to his work with young people is commemorated in the annual prize which bears his name.

ardeners from the Six
lls Nursery, c. 1930. Mr
illiam Nye and Mr Alf
ootton (standing) .

> **Take the underpass which leads from the old Great North Road beneath Six Hills Way. At the underpass T-junction, turn right and then take the second left path marked 'Town Centre'. Follow this route northwards, passing the Court House, the back of the Leisure Centre and continuing to the foot-bridge in Tesco's car-park.**

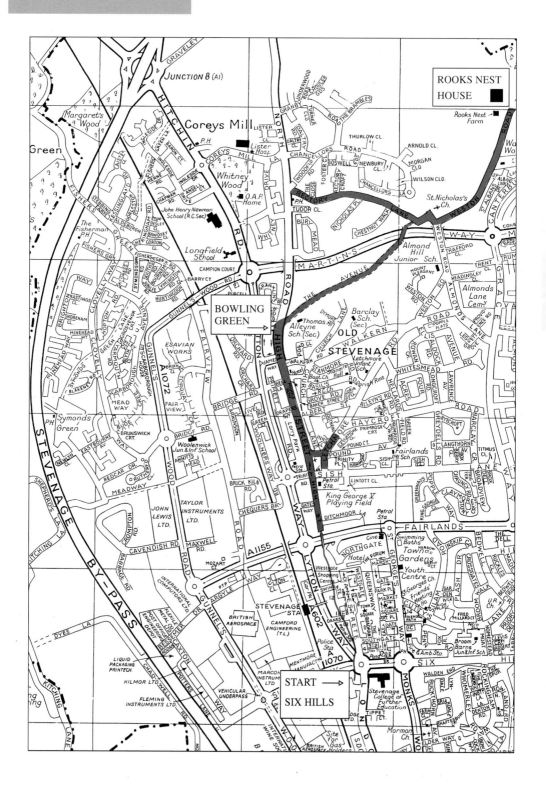

e Guild of Literature and
t, London Road, 1960.

As you walk beneath the modern Six Hills dual carriageway, reflect that near here, 132 years ago, Sir Edward Bulwer Lytton and Charles Dickens proudly attended the opening of their Guild of Arts and Literature; and about here E.M. Forster placed the home of Charles and Dolly Wilcox, in his 1910 novel *Howards End*:

> Charles's house on the left; on the right the swelling forms of the Six Hills. Their appearance in such a neighbourhood surprised her. They interrupted the stream of residences that was thickening up towards Hilton. Beyond them she saw meadows and a wood, and beneath them she settled that soldiers of the best kind lay buried.

Emerging from the underpass, the pedestrian can now rejoin the old Great North Road between the car-park and the site of the recently demolished bus garage (now Kwiksave) and follow it to the Leisure Centre. On the left, across Lytton Way, are the police and railway stations, occupying the site of the old Stevenage football field. On the far side of the railway line, the recently built Kings Park is a reminder that King's Engineering Company previously stood here, a major employer in the small town of Stevenage.

As the old Great North Road passes the Leisure Centre, its Jubilee

posite: Map by courtesy
G.I. Barnett & Son Ltd.
sed upon Ordnance
rvey mapping with the
rmission of the Controller
her Majesty's Stationery
fice, © Crown copyright.

trees and even part of the old hedgerow still remain, reminders of the days when stage-coaches, then cars and lorries, thundered past on their way from London to the north. Now the outdoor market has some of its stalls here.

The Leisure Centre is perhaps one of the most interesting modern buildings in Stevenage. Its controversial exterior orange fibre-glass panels are currently being replaced. Within, it has very up-to-date sports facilities, excellent display facilities for works of art, a restaurant and one of the best designed and most comfortable small theatres for many miles, including London.

The eminent stage designer after whom the theatre is named, Edward Gordon Craig, was born in 1872 at No. 23 Railway Street (now No. 23 Orchard Road), Stevenage, where his mother, Ellen Terry, had come to stay with a midwife for the birth of her child.

Beyond the pedestrian shopping precinct are the town centre gardens, surrounding a small lake which was originally a marshy pond at Bedwell Plash, fed by the spring which has never been stilled. From the Plash, high-hedged Bedwell Lane led down to the Great North Road, past farm buildings and private houses, all of which were demolished to make way for the new town. Watching today's constant stream of cars and pedestrians around the modern town centre buildings, it is difficult to realize that here, along the old road, were Victorian and Edwardian houses such as Woodstone and The White Cottage on the east side, and on the west, among others, The Hermitage – home of Major A. Howard, a member of Stevenage Urban District Council at the time when the new town was in the planning stage.

Climb the steps to the foot-bridge across Fairlands Way before joining the old road again at Ditchmore Lane. Here a diversion is possible, by turning right and following the footpath through the playing fields, to emerge eventually in Sish Lane. However, to follow the route of the Great North Road, continue straight ahead, pausing at the entrance to the King George V Playing Fields opposite the Chequers public house.

The foot-bridge ends at a car-park built on the site of The Firs, home of the Walpole family in the nineteenth century. A brass plate in memory of the Walpoles may be seen in the sanctuary of Holy Trinity church. After the Second World War The Firs was known

The Home Hospital for Women, formerly The Firs, London Road, 1952.

officially as 'The Home Hospital for Women', but the old name refused to die and local people continued to call it The Firs, much to the annoyance of Matron Florence Sugden.

From this point until it joined the High Street, the Great North Road was known as London Road. On its east side was Ditchmore Common, with its row of little Victorian cottages, a stream or ditch running in front and long, narrow gardens behind. One resident kept

Cottages at Ditchmore Common shortly before demolition, c. 1969.

101

pigs in a small adjacent field. A footpath went past, the beginning of a choice of walks to Bedwell Plash, Whomerley Wood or the Six Hills. Now all this is buried under tarmac.

The lane from Ditchmore Common to London Road, for centuries nameless, has recently and quite reasonably acquired the name Ditchmore Lane. But at the same time London Road has been demoted and renamed Ditchmore Lane also.

Continuing along London Road, some Victorian houses still remain on the west side, including No. 6, which has been a veterinary surgeon's for many years. Facing here on the opposite side is the ground of Stevenage Cricket Club, on a site given by Lord Lytton. It is a pleasant ground, shaded on three sides by ancient oak trees and hedgerows, and for most of its life protected by the traditional white paling fence.

To mark the Jubilee of King George V in 1935, additional land was given by Mr Marston Popple for more playing fields. There was an anguished correspondence in the local papers in the 1940s when the council proposed spending public money to plant a hedge round the bowling green. Tennis courts, football pitches and children's swings were added subsequently and the playing fields were extended yet again in the 1950s.

A footpath runs through the King George V Playing Fields from Ditchmore Common to Sish Lane. As it approaches Sish Lane it becomes a crooked, noisome alley, a boarded-up building site on one side and a high brick wall on the other. Until 1068, when it was re-routed, it was a pleasant straight path beside Mr F. Barker's thatched cottage, which had a delightful garden with flowering currant and other shrubs growing over the low boundary wall.

At the main entrance to the playing fields, in London Road, are two brick pillars with heraldic insignia. Unfortunately the approach is currently marred by the adjacent building site which, in previous incarnations, has been a Texas store, Harper's Garage and before that a private house, Swiss Cottage. This was the home of Mr and Mrs Matthews, who owned the printing works in the High Street in the early years of the century.

Opposite is Gates Way, previously Chequers Bridge Road before it was bisected by Lytton Way. The cycle track is built on the former Gates' field, which used to stretch from London Road to the railway line and belonged to the Gates family whose slaughterhouse backed on to it in Trinity Road. Until recently the first in the row of Victorian houses was occupied by Miss Blanche Toll, who continued to light some of her rooms with gas and others with candles until the end of her life. Her brother, Stanley Toll, and his wife lived further along, next door to his funeral business. For many years he was organist at Holy Trinity church. The nearby Chequers public house has a history going back to the eighteenth century, but it has been considerably modernized over the years.

Just beyond the Chequers is a row of most attractive buildings, several of which are of seventeenth-century origin. Until the 1970s the Southend Post Office occupied one cottage, run by Miss Nina Norman. Too small to stock very much in addition to the necessary postage and national savings stamps, it did carry a small selection of stationery and greetings cards. There was a dark brown, wooden shelf, with pen, ink and blotting pad provided, at which customers could stand to write. Immediately behind the door was a large poster warning of the dangers of the Colorado beetle and over the high counter customers caught the occasional glimpse of Miss Norman's sitting-room.

At the end of this row of cottages Trinity Road led from London Road to the railway line. Now vanished under the modern system of flyover and roundabout, this road was extremely wide at the top end, with an open space where cars could park, but as it neared the railway it was filled in with an extra row of houses. There were some ancient lath-and-plaster cottages, including one that had originally been an inn, on the left, on the way down to Gates' slaughterhouse. A little pathway, called Springfield Passage, led to Springfield Cottage (not to be confused with Springfield House in the High Street) and Gates' field. Opposite the slaughterhouse, beside the railway line, was Worboy's (later Gosse's) woodyard and a footpath ran from here parallel to the railway, through fields to Orchard Road. The last few yards still exist behind the gardens of Orchard Crescent.

Continue straight ahead, following the underpass beneath Sish Lane to arrive at the south end of the High Street, outside the Coach and Horses Inn.

Opposite Trinity Road, Sish Lane formerly stopped in a T-junction at the main road, but is now linked by flyover to the Lytton Way roundabout. Named after John Sish, Shish or Shush, a fourteenth-century landowner, Sish Lane used to lead into farmland and the highest point in Stevenage, marked in the middle of a cornfield by a triangulation point. It contains one of the oldest surviving industries in Stevenage, the Stevenage Knitting Company, which still operates from the same small and unobtrusive premises it opened in 1927.

The Methodist church on the corner of Sish Lane and the High Street has changed both its internal and external appearance since it was built in 1876, originally of unfaced brick, with its main entrance in the High Street. The foundation stones are still clearly visible, but the building has been enlarged and a new entrance made in Sish Lane. The internal orientation has also been changed and a large hall and adjacent meeting rooms added. When the one-way system was introduced at each end of the High Street, excavation work was carried on so close to the church that it was in real danger of falling into the builders' hole. Plans were hastily revised and the structure made secure.

The south end of the High Street is rich in history. Until 1861 there was a large pond where Holy Trinity church now stands, and another on the site of B&Q. The latter was drained and the Stevenage Motor Company premises built there in the 1930s next door to the former Ayres Family Grocers' on the corner of Trinity

The south end of the High Street, showing the pond opposite Holy Trinity church. (Painting dated 1896.)

Road. On the other side of the pond, in the early twentieth century, was Shelford's Ideal Bakery and tea-room. The eighteenth-century house beside Game's Garage was probably a former inn or brewhouse. The garage petrol pumps stood directly in front of the house during the Second World War, when convoys of army lorries regularly filled their tanks here. The pumps were moved to new premises when Primett Road was built, in accordance with the Borough Council's policy not to have petrol pumps in the High Street.

Across the road stands Holy Trinity church. The original, 1861 building, designed by Blomfield, is the one with the bell-tower. In 1881 it was more than doubled in size when an extension was added; the church as it is today was completed in 1885, with the building of the chancel and the east window in memory of Dr Andrew Whyte Barclay, of Whitney Wood. The clock was paid for by subscription from parishioners in memory of Canon Blomfield. Before the High Street one-way system was introduced there was a London Transport bus stop outside Holy Trinity and many a traveller would keep an eye on the clock while resting against the church wall.

Turn right past Holy Trinity church and cross Letchmore Road (carefully!) to the Tudor House. Continue past the entrance to Pound Avenue as far as Letchmore Green before crossing Letchmore Road again and returning to the High Street, passing Inns Close and Southend Farm. Pause in the High Street opposite the Marquess of Lorne.

Tudor House, No. 2 Letchmore Road, is the old workhouse, later known as the Gas House and finally, until his death in the 1970s, as Mr Moore's. Eric Moore came to live in Stevenage as manager of the Gas Company, whose enormous gasholders and associated Victorian brick buildings in Sish Lane backed on to his garden. The site is now occupied by the Trinity Close flats. Many Stevenage people today have affectionate memories of Mr Moore as a genial white-haired gentleman with many interests, including ballroom dancing, photography, local history and horology. For many years he kept the Holy Trinity clock in perfect order. His former house has been carefully renovated and now probably looks much as its original builders left it. A replica of the old parish cage, or prison has been built in the grounds.

Incongruously next door to the old workhouse, at the bottom of

The final advertisements for the Astonia Cinema, before it closed on 4 March 1969.

Pound Avenue, is a building in complete contrast. Now used as a snooker club, it was previously a bingo hall, but started life in the 1930s as the Astonia Cinema. From the 1940s to 1970s, the Peugeot car showroom, situated opposite, was the garage of Candler's North Star coaches. Prior to that, the land on which it and the whole road is built, belong to Pound Farm. The farmhouse, pigsty and most outbuildings have now been destroyed, but pigs, chickens and a bull were kept there until the late 1950s. One old barn, now painted white, still remains in Letchmore Road. The position of its hayloft door, high up on the wall, can clearly be seen. The name 'Pound' is taken from the village pound, an enclosure where stray animals were put to prevent them damaging crops. Another pound existed at some time at Pin Green, which was originally 'Pynd' or 'Pound' Green.

On the way back to the High Street is Southend Farm, of great architectural interest. It is a genuine Wealden hall house with all its features preserved. Until the 1960s it retained some of its fields, where Inns Close and Southend Close have since been built. The rural nature of Stevenage was such that, until this time, Mr George Lines daily walked his cows from the farmyard at No. 124 High Street (the present site of the Vauxhall Motor showrooms) into the meadow at Southend Farm and back again in the afternoon.

The space between Holy Trinity church, Southend Farm and the beginning of the High Street was for much of the nineteenth century the Stevenage straw plait market, where local people, mainly women and children, gathered to sell their plait to dealers. Often they also acquired the particular type of straw, known as Lammas, at the market. Once the new town hall was built in 1871, the market moved indoors.

No. 129 High Street is still known to many as Steers' Corner. In the 1920s and '30s it was a restaurant or roadhouse and particularly well known to the parties of cyclists who used to ride out from London on day trips into the country. At one time there was fierce competition between Steers and the Marquess of Lorne opposite, the two establishments each resorting to devious tricks to entice trade.

The High Street from this point on is so crowded with old buildings, each having its own history, that it is impossible to mention everything of interest. Detailed information can be found in 'The Changing Face of Stevenage High Street', published by the Stevenage Society. Even in recent years there have been immense changes in the use and occupancy of the buildings; where there was a range of small shops, each selling something different, now there are very few. Offices, estate agencies and eating-places have predominated in recent years. But change is continuous. The shops and businesses of the early twentieth century took over the run-down coaching inns of a previous age, as the many High Street buildings with wide entrance archways indicate. They themselves had replaced the former old wooden buildings which had succumbed to fire and decay.

Walk along the High Street, crossing as necessary to look at points of interest. Note, the odd numbers are on the east side and the even numbers on the west. Continue in a northerly direction, passing Shepherd's Path, which links the High Street to Church Lane. Pause at Albert Street.

Next to the old Steers restaurant, Nos. 123 and 125 High Street were, in the nineteenth century, a public house, the George and Dragon, owned in its latter years by Simpsons, the Baldock brewers. A cellar full of empty bottles was found there during renovations in the 1960s. For most of this century No. 115 was Boorman's cycle shop. Next door, No. 113 has seen many changes: it was one of the row of cottages occupied by J. Titmus (wheelwright), Mary Mead (needlewoman) and J. Red (agricultural labourer) in the 1870s; in the 1920s it was briefly the town Labour Exchange, managed by Mr F. Archer; it became a greengrocer's, occupied first by the Welch family in the 1930s and '40s, and then by Richard and Merle Tompson; and it is now the studio of Kingsley Michael, photographer.

The White Hart public house is almost certainly the inn which Dickens called the Peal of Bells in his story *Tom Tiddler's Ground*. From its windows, in 1861, Dickens looked out to the opposite side of the High Street towards No. 106, which is probably the building he referred to as 'the attorney's red brick house'. It may or may not have been occupied by a lawyer at that date, but it was certainly the home of Dr J.B.B. Connell in the 1830s and of S. Chittenden, a member of the Stock Exchange, in the 1870s.

Between the White Hart and the Unicorn in the 1930s and '40s was a variety of shops, including 'Fishy' Furr's fishmonger's, at No. 97, G. Sharpe's shop, which dealt in shoe repairs, small leather goods, stationery, meccano and a miscellany of other goods, at No. 93 and the wonderful toy shop of Lewin Waby at No. 91. Although very tiny, it drew local children like a magnet, and they would gaze longingly at the window display crowded with model farmyard animals, dolls, clockwork cars and other desirables. The

Mrs M. Tompson in her greengrocer's shop, *c.* 1985.

A pipe band outside the Unicorn public house, playing for the New Year's Eve celebrations.

The former saddlery, with three steps, next to the Red Lion, one of the oldest inns in Stevenage, 1975.

Unicorn (previously the Fox) was at Nos. 77 to 79, now the Bombay Restaurant. During the 1960s the publican led a thriving Stevenage Pipe Band and often the sound of bagpipes could be heard from the Unicorn's backyard in Church Lane.

Opposite, No. 82 is a most intriguing building. Currently an antique shop, it was previously a saddler's, as its high steps indicate. In the 1830s it was part of a group of farm buildings and was occupied by George Gayler, saddler and harness-maker, who was still there in the 1870s. The last saddler to ply his trade here was Mr W. Allison, a spruce figure, girt about with leather apron, who was one of the last people in the town to travel by pony and trap. His smart turnout and the clip-clop of his horse's hooves cheered the High Street until the 1970s. The Red Lion next door has a history going back at least to the sixteenth century. A.G. Lines, ironmonger, at No. 76, has been in the same family for most of this century. Previously it was Silk's and in the 1870s it was owned by T. Briden and occupied by R. Toll, a builder.

Draper's Way was formerly Green Street, leading to a foot-bridge over the railway. During the nineteenth century, a house and farm buildings owned by F.P. Delme Radcliffe of Hitchin Priory, a well-known Master of Fox Hounds, stood on the site of Green Street. The house was occupied by Richard Whittington, who also owned No. 72, which later became a large draper's and general store, owned by J. Green, after whom Green Street was named. No. 72 continued as a draper's when it changed hands and became Henderson's, hence the name Draper's Way for this part of Green Street, when it was cut off from the rest by the construction of Lytton Way. The modern Waitrose store now occupies the site of the old draper's shop.

Opposite, on the east side of the High Street, is Albert Street, now almost entirely residential following its redevelopment in the 1960s. Before then it contained a variety of premises: a Baptist chapel; a photographic studio run first by A.W. Middleton then by Percy Howard; drapers' shops; a tobacconist; a hairdresser; a grocer; Hutchinson's bakery, with its delivery horse stabled immediately next door; Chittenden's furniture shop; blind Mr Fletcher's hardware store; and many others, interspersed with the cottages fronting directly on to the street.

Nos. 10 to 12, occupied by Joseph Findley, included a barber's shop, a tobacconist and confectioner's and a shop specializing in umbrella and picture frame making, run by his brother, John. In the 1930s one shop was let to Mr Presland, a television and radio

Mr Phipps with milk-float,
outside the Chequers,
London Road, in 1946.

engineer. The black and white television set in the window attracted
many a passer-by. Many corner shops in Albert Street were
conversions of the front rooms of dwelling houses and a very wide
variety of businesses was carried on here during the 1930s.

At the corner of Church Lane was Phipps' Dairy, with a low brick
wall round the garden and stabling for the horse and cart. Church Lane
itself has been widened and tidied up. The straggly hawthorn hedges,
old barns and flint cottages are now but a memory, as is the blacksmith's
forge. The horse-chestnut tree which stood in the yard still remains,
however, as do parts of the footpath which ran from the High Street,
beside the Stevenage Printing Works, past the forge and through the
fields and gardens into Letchmore Green. The last blacksmith, William
Shepherd, and his family are immortalized in the name Shepherd's Path.

**From the Albert Street junction continue northwards along the
High Street, east side. Look at Norfolk House, No. 65, and the
newsagents, No. 63, before walking through Middle Row, where
the commercial centre of Stevenage began during the Middle
Ages.**

Here itinerant tradesmen set up their stalls and booths, at first on a
temporary basis then gradually making them more permanent until
shops and dwelling places became established. The tall building,
Norfolk House, currently Simmond's the bakers, was a butcher's
shop for over one hundred years.

The black and white building next door, Nos. 61 and 63, was, in 1870, the Stevenage Post Office, occupied by postmaster T. Smith. Today it is still remembered by some people as Chambers' Library. In the early years of the twentieth century it was occupied by H.J. Chambers, bookseller, stationer and newsagent, who also ran a small commercial lending library and operated as the Stevenage branch office of the *Hertfordshire Express* newspaper. In an advertisement of December 1904, the paper's proprietors, William Carling and Co. of Hitchin, proclaimed:

> From this date onwards the interest of the *Express* in Stevenage will be in the care of Mr H.J. Chambers as our correspondent and chief distributing agent. Mr Chambers, who is a shorthand writer and expert journalist, has become tenant of the very central and convenient premises in the High Street, lately occupied by Mr Charles Munro.

The connection with the press remains today, No. 63 continuing as a newsagents and No. 61, until recently, as the office of the *Stevenage Gazette*, successor to the *Hertfordshire Express*.

In the days before public libraries became established it was commonplace for shops and private individuals to run subscription libraries and there were several of these in Stevenage in the first half of the twentieth century. In the 1940s and '50s No. 67a was the Hills Home Library. It was a tiny but delightful storehouse, full of most enjoyable, if not necessarily of 'approved' reading matter, crammed from floor to ceiling with Richmal Crompton's *William* books, Enid Blyton stories, thrillers, romances and westerns.

The buildings in Middle Row have seen many changes of owners and use over the centuries. Despite superficial changes, however, many have retained their sixteenth-century structures; others may have even earlier origins. They were fortunate to escape the eighteenth-century fires, which destroyed so much of the High Street, and therefore avoided the rebuilding that followed. Among the stream of trades which has come and gone in Middle Row over the centuries it is worth mentioning the public house with the unusual name of The Buckingham Palace at No. 9a. It finally closed its doors in 1919, and little is known of its history. Opposite, until the 1970s, was Halling's spotlessly clean butcher's shop, with its fresh paintwork and bright window-boxes.

At the top of Middle Row, at No. 37 High Street, stands the

e Buckingham Palace
blic house, No. 9A Middle
ow, in 1910.

National Westminster Bank, formerly the Old Castle Inn, where Henry Trigg lived in the eighteenth century. The instructions in his will that his body should not be buried but placed on the rafters of his barn, were faithfully carried out, making the Old Castle something of a tourist attraction. The last publican of the inn was George Gray, who moved to Trinity Road in the 1920s.

> **Continue northwards along the High Street, crossing the road as appropriate. Pause outside the public library at No. 38.**

The High Street widens out noticeably between the White Lion and the National Westminster Bank (formerly the Old Castle Inn). Before the road was surfaced and footpaths paved, this large open space was the town's market-place, used largely for cattle which drank from the ponds behind the White Lion. When the cattle markets were no longer held and the pavements had been laid, the space on the east side continued, spasmodically, to be used for market stalls for a variety of goods until the 1960s when a market was opened in the new town centre.

Behind the old market-place, Nos. 35 (currently R.J. Pratt & Son, TV specialists), 33 (Lloyds Bank) and 31 (Stevenage Club and Institute) have an interesting history. Their owners in the nineteenth century seem to have exchanged properties with one another. In the 1830s No. 35 was a house and yard owned by Isabella Muncey, No. 33 was a house and garden belonging to Alice Fisher, who ran a ladies' boarding school there, and No. 31 was owned by butcher Joseph Moulden. By the 1870s No. 35 had become Mary Fisher's school, while Joseph Moulden had moved his butcher's shop to No. 33 and G. Moules, a farmer employing six men and two boys, lived at No. 31.

No. 35 continued as a school until the early years of the twentieth century, with Miss Louisa Beaver as headmistress. She had previously lived and taught at No. 61 and was no doubt glad to move into more spacious premises. By 1937 No. 35 was being used by H.J. Hutchinson, whose bakery was in Albert Street, as a shop and cafe famed for its vanilla slices and cream cornets. No. 33 remained a butcher's shop until the late 1930s, owned by the O'Clee family who took over from Joseph Moulden.

The Cromwell Hotel, lately renamed the Stevenage Moathouse, is thought by some to have begun its life as a farmhouse and to have had connections with Oliver Cromwell's Secretary of State, John

Thurloe. Known in the early years of this century as Cromwell Lodge, it was then owned by the Corbould-Ellis family, one of whom was a respected artist. When it became a hotel in the 1930s it achieved a good reputation among travellers and was proud to claim the eminent musician Sir Henry Wood as one of its regular visitors. The gardens, which used to stretch to the line of lime trees in the centre of Walkern Road, were designed by Clarence Elliott and were a most charming feature of the High Street, with a particularly attractive fish-pond, illuminated at night. Regrettably, when the new road system was introduced, a large slice of these delightful gardens was removed. No. 27, now part of the hotel and called Oliver's, was used from the 1930s to the 1950s by the Hertfordshire County Council as a welfare clinic for mothers and babies. The dreaded school dentist and the Red Cross were also housed there for a time.

On the opposite side of the road, the Taj Mahal restaurant, No. 70, currently occupies the house formerly known as The Rookery, where in the early twentieth century Madame Hatton-Edwards held her dancing classes. One of her most enthusiastic and talented pupils was the young Elizabeth Poston, who was to become a great composer and musician. Incongruously, by 1937, The Rookery had become the premises of the Tottenham and District Gas Company.

The White Lion Hotel formerly stood beside an open space, through which cattle could be driven into the fields behind and where stage-coaches could unload, as the White Lion's entrance archway was too low to allow them through into the yard. When Stevenage began to organize its fire brigades more efficiently, in the

Young dancers in the garden of the Rookery, Madame Hatton Edwards' School of Dancing, No. 70 High Street, 1905.

nineteenth century, they needed a centrally positioned fire bell which could be heard by volunteers at work in or near the High Street. The space beside the White Lion was well suited to this purpose and in 1887 a brick bell-turret was built there. However, in 1905 a new road bridge over the railway was built, to replace the old foot-bridge in Green Street. In order to make way for Bridge Road, the bell-turret was demolished; in any case, the fire brigade by this time had its premises in Basil's Road, on the corner of Church Lane. Bridge Road was another victim of Lytton Way, the High Street end of it now being renamed Bell Lane.

From the late 1930s to the 1960s the Stevenage branch of Woolworth's was situated at No. 50 (now Elmes Arcade). It was then transferred to the new town centre. Another household name, Boots the Chemist, has retained its old town branch at No. 54, which has been a chemist's shop since at least 1870 when it was owned by Lewis Fresson, who was prominent in the affairs of the town. In 1887 a new post office was opened at No. 52.

The Hertfordshire Library Service currently occupies No. 38. Previously it was the Eastern Electricity Showroom (and before that the North Metropolitan Electricity Board). In the early nineteenth century it was used for religious worship by the Methodist congregation in Stevenage. Now demolished, No. 32 used to be a watchmaker's shop on the corner of Orchard Road, occupied for much of this century by W. Bickell and before that by S. James, hence the name James Way for the road which is built over it. Formerly, Orchard Road started from this point of the High Street and curved round to the railway station in Julian's Road. It housed the town hall, council offices and the little county library branch, where Doris Baker was librarian. A footpath between the library and Orchard Court ran through the fields behind the High Street.

> **Take the underpass in front of the library and cross beneath James Way, to emerge outside Springfield House. Follow the path past the Bowling Green and war memorial and continue to the underpass which leads from behind the Bowling Green houses, under the main road, to The Avenue. Walk a few yards south to the Grange.**

Springfield House, facing the Bowling Green, was owned in the nineteenth century by the Revd John Osborne Seager, curate of the parish and Master of Alleyne's Grammar School until he founded the Grange School almost next door. In the twentieth century Springfield House was owned for many years by Jeremiah Inns, the hay and corn dealer, who became a millionaire. During the Second World War he and his wife Helen were particularly hospitable to the Stevenage Home Guard. In his will, Jeremiah Inns left money to build the almshouses at Inns Close, off Letchmore Road, and he gave Springfield House to the town. It is now the Old Stevenage Community Association premises and also houses the Denington Art Gallery, named after Dame Evelyn Denington, one-time Chairman of the Stevenage Development Corporation, and administered by the Artists' Co-operative. A modern piece of sculpture which previously stood in the town centre is now on view in the gardens.

The Poplars, No. 6, is still remembered with affection by many as 'Miss Grosvenor's', the home for many years of Dorothy Grosvenor, daughter of Dr Grosvenor, whose surgery was at No. 66. Miss Grosvenor was very attached to the old town of Stevenage and a founder member of the Stevenage Society. She kept a scrapbook of local history, which she left to the museum on her death. She was a character, unstuffy, slightly eccentric and full of fun to the end. Next to her house was Field's Dairy, now obliterated by a cycle track. The small building currently used by the Florist on the Green was originally a blacksmith's forge.

During the 1930s, '40s and '50s the black and white building of the Publix Cinema stood at the top of the Bowling Green, regarded with a mixture of affection and exasperation by patrons who waited impatiently when the projector broke down, or the film was repaired yet again. The Bowling Green itself has been much cut about and tidied up in recent years. It began life as an untidy village green at the point where the High Street forked, one road going to Hitchin, the other, North Road, sometimes called Baldock Road, being a continuation of the Great North Road. A public drinking fountain used to stand on the green near Hawkes' Shoe Shop, at No. 30, but was removed to make way for the underpass beneath James Way. The war memorial was erected and dedicated in 1921 and it was not long after this that the main part of the green was fenced around. George ('Bones') Ellis, who was then employed at the ESA, was one of those who put up the fencing posts and chains.

Across the North Road stands the Grange, once the famous Swan Inn. Since its coaching days it has had a varied career, first as the Grange School, under the headmastership of the Revd John Osborne

Seager, succeeded by his son, the Revd John Lingen Seager. In 1893 young E.M. Forster boarded here for less than a month, and suffered unforgettable misery. During the Second World War the Grange became home to the children of Briar Patch Children's Home, whose Letchworth premises had been destroyed by fire. After the war it was taken over by Hertfordshire County Council. Part of it is now used as the Stevenage Registry Office. The pillars under the front portico came from St Nicholas' church, where they supported a gallery at the west end. They were removed in the nineteenth century as part of Canon Blomfield's alterations.

The old maltings, next to the Thomas Alleyne School, 197: In the 1940s and '50s this wa: the home of Vincent HRD motor cycles.

The blue heritage plaque on the attractive black and white building next to Alleyne's school is not to be believed. This building is in fact a fifteenth-century maltings. It was used during the 1930s and '40s as the premises of the Vincent HRD Company, which manufactured world famous motor cycles, including the Black Shadow, upon which Mr Brown, of the shop in the High Street, rode to world record speeds. The maltings was not, as the text proclaims, part of Alleyne's school. The original schoolhouse is the small building just inside the main school gates, on the left, next to The Avenue. The school itself is now co-educational and has changed its name to the Thomas Alleyne School.

> **Return to The Avenue and walk the whole of its length, including the foot-bridge over Martin's Way, to arrive in Rectory Lane. Here a diversion may be made by turning left and walking down Rectory Lane as far as its junction with North Road, then returning to the top of Rectory Lane and St Nicholas' church.**

Entering The Avenue today is not quite the pleasure it once was. The memorial gates are gone, as are many of the ancient trees, blown down in the great storm of 1987, or felled because of disease. The old St Nicholas' Primary School (the National School) has also been demolished, except for the schoolhouse, with its bell-turret as a reminder of its original use. Two modern houses, the vicarage for St Nicholas' church and the former home of Eric Claxton, Chief Engineer to the Stevenage Development Corporation, have been built on the old school site and a cycle track enters what used to be the school playground. The days when cycling and horse-riding were strictly forbidden have long since gone and pedestrians have to be on the alert.

The Bury Mead and the playing fields of the Alleyne's and Barclay schools provide a welcome vista of green, but the drone of traffic is ever present since The Avenue was cut in two for the building of Martin's Way. A spiralling pedestrian foot-bridge replaces the trees which, in this section, were planted in 1935 to mark the Jubilee of King George V and Queen Mary. The board commemorating this has been destroyed by the ubiquitous 'vandals'. The Stevenage Borough Council, which now manages The Avenue on lease from the Church of England, has done an excellent job of replanting, using young trees donated by British Aerospace, and maintaining verges in an environmentally sound way, allowing grasses to grow up and seed, thus providing food and shelter for wildlife. The Council has also recently resurfaced the path with traditional hoggin.

The Avenue leads into Rectory Lane, now devoid of the building which gave it its name. The last rectory, which was built in 1919 when Canon Molony was rector, stood on the site which Chestnut Walk now occupies. Before 1919, for over three hundred years, the building half-way down Rectory Lane and now known as the Priory, was home to the rectors of Stevenage. Before that, in the eighteenth century or earlier, the religious foundation which supported the church was probably further down the lane, at Woodfield, which is now a residential home. At the junction of Rectory Lane and the North Road the house named Turnpike Close is a reminder of the turnpike toll-house which stood near here. The Marquess of Granby (now the Granby) public house on the corner and the milestone a hundred yards further down the North Road, towards Stevenage, are other links with the coaching era.

Returning to the top of Rectory Lane, the walker now arrives at the heart of the Saxon village of Stigenace. Here, on the site of St Nicholas' church and the Old Bury, is where Stevenage began. The church building and the tombstones and monuments in the churchyard are rich sources of local history and repay repeated visits to study them. A footpath leads through the churchyard into open countryside known the world over as the Forster Country. Here the walker may stride out to the deserted village of Chesfield, with its ruined church of St Etheldreda and its superb view of Graveley and the distant Chiltern hills from the Ledgeside plantation, or take a slightly different route to emerge at the charming group of cottages at Crow End. From St Nicholas' churchyard, the way is open to the Hertfordshire countryside

The Avenue, after the great storm of 1987.

which, in the words of E.M. Forster, has 'nothing special about it' but is yet 'the loveliest in England'.

> **Spend some time exploring the church (directions for obtaining the key are on the notice-board) and churchyard, then leave by the lych-gate or one of the paths into Weston Road and proceed towards Weston, pausing at Rooks Nest. Do not confuse Rooks Nest Farm with Rooks Nest House, a few yards further on.**

The old road to Weston leads past St Nicholas' and two adjacent cottages, to the hamlet of Rooks Nest. Building development is going on apace and there is now a cul-de-sac where Rooks Nest Farm and Rooks Nest House stand. Centuries ago there were two farms, known as Upper and Lower Rooks Nest. Then Upper Rooks Nest became known as Howard's or Mr Howard's after the family which lived there for over three hundred years, until they left in 1882 and the property was acquired by the Wilkinsons of Chesfield Park. Why the Howards left and where they went is still not known.

In 1883 a young widow, Mrs Lily Forster, brought her four-year-old son, Edward Morgan Forster, to live at Rooks Nest House and he loved it so much that 'I wished I could stay there for ever'. Sadly, he and his mother had to leave in 1893, but Forster immortalized the place in his novel *Howards End*, published in 1910 and made into a film in 1992. From 1914 to 1987 Rooks Nest House was the home of Elizabeth Poston, composer of the much-loved carol 'Jesus Christ the Apple Tree' and many other works.

Shephall Village

The building of Stevenage New Town has engulfed the ancient village of Shephall, which is now considered one of the 'neighbourhoods'. The church of St Mary, the Red Lion Inn, the village green and surrounding cottages remain, accessible by car from Hydean Way or by foot via the underpass from Shephalbury Park. Those who are interested in finding out more of the long history of this attractive village are urged to obtain a copy of Mary Spicer's *Tyme Out of Mind*.

Further Reading

Places of publication are given only if outside London.

Amess, John, *Stevenage at War, 1939–45.* Stevenage Museum Publications, 1987.

Appleton, Maggie, *Stevenage in Old Photographs.* Stroud, Alan Sutton Publishing, 1993.

Davies, E. St Hill and Dodwell, F., *Hidden from History: women in Stevenage, 1888–1988.* Stevenage Borough Council.

Chauncy, Sir Henry, *Historical Antiquities of Hertfordshire.* 1700.

Gover, J.E.B., *The Place-names of Hertfordshire.* Cambridge University Press, 1938.

Harding, Eileen, *Brignall, White and Orchard, solicitors.* Stevenage, St George's Chambers, The Forum, 1987.

Johnson, W. Branch, *Hertfordshire.* Batsford, 1970.

Lack, G.L., *Stevenage street names.* Letchworth, Focus Publications, 1974.

Mullan, Bob, *Stevenage Ltd.* Routledge & Kegan Paul, 1980.

Munby, Lionel, *The Hertfordshire Landscape.* Hodder & Stoughton Ltd, 1977.

Rees, Huw and Connie, *The History Makers.* Stevenage, 1991.

Spicer, C.M, *Tyme Out of Mind.* Stevenage, 1984.

Stevenage Parish Magazine, 1871-1917.

Stevenage Society, *The Changing Face of Stevenage High Street.* Stevenage Museum Publications, 1982.

Trow-Smith, Robert, *The History of Stevenage.* Stevenage Society, 1958.

Viatores, *Roman Roads in the south-east Midlands.* Gollancz, 1964.

As well as the title listed above, the Stevenage Society has produced various other highly recommended publications. There are excellent and well-managed collections of material about Stevenage and district in the Stevenage Museum, the Stevenage Library, the Hertfordshire Library Service Local History Section and the Hertfordshire County Record Office.

Acknowledgements and Picture Credits

I am grateful to the many people who helped and encouraged me in the writing of this book, especially:

Maggie Appleton, my father J.V. Ashby, Denis Boorman, Peter Boorman, Len Brown, Wendy Brodie-Waghorn, Joyce Emery, Roy Findley, Betty Game, Mrs L. Game, Ralph Game, Anne Haines, Joan Hale, John Hepworth, Julia Holberry and her staff at Stevenage Museum, Bob Hooper, Margery and Philip Ireton, Joan Jeffery, Valerie Lines, Nellie Manning, June Pitcher, Ken Poole, Jim Poston, Arthur Richards, the staff of the Hertfordshire County Record Office, the staff of the Hertfordshire Library Service – and Dougal, for waiting patiently.

Every effort has been made to trace copyright owners and obtain their permission to reproduce the illustrations included in this book. If there are any errors or omissions I apologize to those concerned and ask their forbearance.

I gratefully acknowledge the following for kindly granting me permission to reproduce the illustrations:

G.L. Blake, p. 99; Echo & Post Ltd, p. 95; Betty Game, front cover, p. 96; Mrs L. Game, pp. 76 (top), 77 (top), 104; Ralph Game, p. 90; Grange Publishing, p. 101 (top); *Hertfordshire Pictorial*, pp. 79 (bottom), 91 (top), 92, 94; Bob Hooper, p. 89 (bottom); Philip Ireton, p. 91 (bottom); Lea Valley Dairies, p. 110; Mr J.N. and Mrs E.J. Tomkins, p. 84; James Poston, p. 68 (top); Diocese of St Albans, p. 93; *Stevenage Gazette*, pp. 46, 106, 108 (bottom); Stevenage Museum: pp. vi, 3, 5, 7, 10, 12, 19, 26, 39, 45, 47, 49, 54, 58, 59, 67, 68 (bottom), 70, 71, 73, 75 (bottom), 76 (bottom), 79 (top), 82, 88, 89 (top), 97, 101 (bottom), 111, 113; Mrs Tomlin, p. 77 (bottom).

All other photographs used remain the property of the author.

ndex